LEGENDS OF THE BASTILLE

MODEL OF THE BASTILE, CARVED IN ONE OF THE STONES OF THE FORTRESS.

One of these models, made by the instructions of the architect Palloy, was sent to the chief-town of every department in France.

Legends of the Bastille

BY

FRANTZ FUNCK-BRENTANO

WITH AN INTRODUCTION BY VICTORIEN SARDOU

AUTHORISED TRANSLATION BY
GEORGE MAIDMENT

WITH EIGHT ILLUSTRATIONS

Fredonia Books
Amsterdam, The Netherlands

Legends of the Bastille

by
Frantz Funck-Brentano

ISBN: 1-4101-0437-0

Copyright © 2004 by Fredonia Books

Reprinted from the 1899 edition

Fredonia Books
Amsterdam, The Netherlands
http://www.fredoniabooks.com

All rights reserved, including the right to reproduce this book, or portions thereof, in any form.

In order to make original editions of historical works available to scholars at an economical price, this facsimile of the original edition of 1899 is reproduced from the best available copy and has been digitally enhanced to improve legibility, but the text remains unaltered to retain historical authenticity.

TRANSLATOR'S PREFACE

In his own entertaining way, Mr. Andrew Lang has recently been taking the scientific historian to task, and giving him a very admirable lesson on " history as she ought to be wrote." But though the two professors to whom he mainly addresses himself are Frenchmen, it would be doing an injustice to France to infer that she is the *alma mater* of the modern dryasdust. The exact contrary is the case : France is rich in historical writers like the Comte d'Haussonville, M. de Maulde la Clavière, M. Gaston Boissier, to name only a few, who know how to be accurate without being dull.

M. Funck-Brentano, whom I have the honour of introducing here to the English public, belongs to the same class. Of literary parentage and connections—his uncle is Professor Lujo Brentano, whose work on the English trade gilds is a standard—he entered in his twentieth year the École des Chartes, the famous institution which trains men in the methods of historical research. At the end of his three years' course, he was appointed to succeed François Ravaisson in the work of classifying the archives of the Bastille in the Arsenal Library,—a work which occupied him for more than ten years. One fruit of it is to be seen in the huge catalogue of more than one thousand pages, printed under official auspices and awarded the Prix Le Dissez de Penanrum by the Académie des Sciences morales et politiques. Another is the present work, which has been crowned by the French Academy. Meanwhile M. Funck-Brentano had been pursuing his studies at the Sorbonne and at Nancy, and his French thesis for the doctorate in letters was a volume on the origins of the Hundred Years' War, which obtained for him the highest possible distinction for a work of erudition in France, the Grand Prix Gobert. This volume he intends to follow up with two others, completing a social rather than a military history of the war, and this no doubt he regards as his *magnum opus*. He is known also as a lecturer in Belgium and Alsace as well as in Paris, and being general secretary of the Société des Etudes historiques and deputy professor of history at the College of France as well as sub-librarian of the Arsenal Library, he leads a busy life.

Trained in the rigorous methods of the École des Chartes and inspired by the examples of Fustel de Coulanges and M. Paul Meyer, M. Funck-Brentano has developed a most interesting and conscientious method of his own. He depends on original sources, and subjects these to the most searching critical tests; but this is a matter of course: his individuality appears in regard to the publication of the results of his researches. When he has discoveries of importance to communicate, he gives them to the world first in the form of articles or studies in reviews of standing, thus preparing public opinion, and at the same time affording opportunities for the search-light of criticism to play on his work. Some of the chapters of this book thus appeared in the various *revues*, and have subsequently gone through a severe process of pruning and amending. It is now eleven years since the first appearance, in the pages of the *Revue des deux Mondes*, of the study of Latude which, in a much altered shape, now forms one of the most interesting portions of this book. The coming autumn will see the publication in France of a striking work by M. Funck-Brentano on the amazing poison-dramas at Louis XIV.'s court, and of this book also the several sections have been appearing at intervals for several years past.

The present work, as I have already said, is the fruit of many years of research. Its startling revelations, so well summarized in M. Victorien Sardou's Introduction, have revolutionized public opinion in France, and in particular the solution of the old problem of the identity of the Man in the Iron Mask has been accepted as final by all competent critics. The *Athenæum*, in reviewing the book in its French form the other day, said that it must be taken cautiously as an ingenious bit of special pleading, and that the Bastille appears in M. Funck-Brentano's pages in altogether too roseate hues, suggesting further that no such results could be obtained without prejudice from the same archives as those on which Charpentier founded his *La Bastille dévoilée* in 1789. This criticism seems to me to ignore several important points. Charpentier's book, written in the heat of the revolutionary struggle, is not a history, but a political pamphlet, which, in the nature of the case, was bound to represent the Bastille as a horror. Moreover, Charpentier could only have depended superficially on the archives, which, as M. Funck-Brentano shows, were thrown into utter disorder on the day of the capture of the Bastille. The later writer, on the other hand, approached the subject when the revolutionary ardours had quite burnt out, and with the independent and dispassionate mind of a trained official. He spent thirteen years in setting the rediscovered archives in order, after his predecessor Ravaisson had already spent a considerable time at the same work. He was able, further (as Charpentier certainly was not), to complete and check the testimony of the archives by means of the memoirs of prisoners—the Abbé Morellet, Marmontel, Renneville, Dumouriez, and a host of others. In these circumstances it would be surprising if his conclusions were not somewhat different from those of Charpentier a hundred years ago.

The gravamen of the *Athenæum's* objection is that M. Funck-Brentano's description of the treatment of prisoners in the Bastille applies only to the favoured few, the implication being that M. Funck-Brentano has shut his eyes to the cases of the larger number. But surely the reviewer must have read the book too rapidly. M. Funck-Brentano shows, by means of existing and accessible documents, that the fact of being sent to the Bastille at all was itself, in the eighteenth century at least, a mark of favour. Once at the Bastille, the prisoner, whoever he might be, was treated without severity, unless he misbehaved. Prisoners of no social importance, such as Renneville, Latude (a servant's love-child), Tavernier (son of a house-porter), were fed and clothed and cared for much better than they would have been outside the prison walls. A young man named Estival de Texas, who was being exiled to Canada because he was a disgrace to his family, wrote to the minister of Paris on June 22, 1726, from the roadstead of La Rochelle: "Your lordship is sending me to a wild country, huddled with mean wretches, and condemned to a fare very different from what your lordship granted me in the Bastille." Here was a friendless outcast looking back regretfully on his prison fare! On February 6, 1724, one of the king's ministers wrote to the lieutenant of

TRANSLATOR'S PREFACE

police : "I have read to the duke of Bourbon the letter you sent me about the speeches of M. Quéhéon, and his royal highness has instructed me to send you an order and a *lettre de cachet* authorizing his removal to the Bastille. But as he thinks that this is *an honour the fellow little deserves*, he wishes you to postpone the execution of the warrant for three days, in order to see if Quéhéon will not take the hint and leave Paris as he was commanded." It is on such documents as these, which are to be seen in hundreds at the Arsenal Library in Paris, that M. Funck-Brentano has founded his conclusions. Anyone who attacks him on his own ground is likely to come badly off.

With M. Funck-Brentano's permission, I have omitted the greater part of his footnotes, which are mainly references to documents inaccessible to the English reader. On the other hand, I have ventured to supply a few footnotes in explanation of such allusions as the Englishman not reading French (and the translation is intended for no others) might not understand. On the same principle I have attempted rhymed renderings of two or three scraps of verse quoted from Regnier and Voltaire, to whom I make my apologies. The proofs have had the advantage of revision by M. Funck-Brentano, who is, however, in no way responsible for any shortcomings. The Index appears in the English version alone.

The portrait of Latude and the views of the Bastille are reproduced from photographs of the originals specially taken by M. A. Bresson, of 40 Rue de Passy, Paris.

GEORGE MAIDMENT.

August, 1899.

CONTENTS

	PAGE
INTRODUCTION	1

CHAPTER I.
THE ARCHIVES 47

CHAPTER II.
HISTORY OF THE BASTILLE 57

CHAPTER III.
LIFE IN THE BASTILLE 85

CHAPTER IV.
THE MAN IN THE IRON MASK 114

CHAPTER V.
MEN OF LETTERS IN THE BASTILLE . . . 147
   I. VOLTAIRE 148
   II. LA BEAUMELLE 152
   III. THE ABBÉ MORELLET 155

Contents

Men of Letters in the Bastille (*cont.*)—

	PAGE
IV. MARMONTEL	158
V. LINGUET	163
VI. DIDEROT	165
VII. THE MARQUIS DE MIRABEAU	166

CHAPTER VI.

Latude 168

CHAPTER VII.

The Fourteenth of July 238

Index 277

LIST OF ILLUSTRATIONS

Model of the Bastille	. . . . . .	*Frontispiece*
Facsimile of Du Junca's note regarding the entry of the Iron Mask	. . .	*Facing page* 115
Facsimile of Du Junca's note regarding the death of the Iron Mask	. . .	,, 116
Facsimile of the Iron Mask's burial certificate		,, 142
Facsimile of the cover of Latude's explosive box	. . . .	,, 173
Facsimile of Latude's writing with blood on linen	. . . . . .	,, 188
Portrait of Latude	. . . . .	,, 229
The Capture of the Bastille	. . .	,, 257

INTRODUCTION

AT the great Exhibition of 1889 I visited, in company with some friends, the reproduction of the Bastille, calculated to give all who saw it—and the whole world must have seen it—an entirely false impression.

You had barely cleared the doorway when you saw, in the gloom, an old man enveloped in a long white beard, lying on the "sodden straw" of tradition, rattling his chains and uttering doleful cries. And the guide said to you, not without emotion, "You see here the unfortunate Latude, who remained in this position, with both arms thus chained behind his back, for thirty-five years!"

This information I completed by adding in the same tone: "And it was in this attitude that he so cleverly constructed the ladder, a hundred and eighty feet long, which enabled him to escape."

The company looked at me with surprise, the guide with a scowl, and I slipped away.

The same considerations that prompted my intervention have suggested to M. Funck-Brentano this work on the Bastille, in which he has set the facts in their true light, and confronted the legends which everyone knows with the truth of which many are in ignorance.

For in spite of all that has been written on the subject by Ravaisson, in the introduction to his *Archives of the Bastille*, by Victor Fournel, in his *Men of the Fourteenth of July*, and by other writers, the popular idea of the internal administration of the Bastille in 1789 holds by the description of Louis Blanc: " Iron cages, recalling Plessis-les-Tours [1] and the tortures of Cardinal La Balue ! [2]—underground dungeons, the loathsome haunts of toads, lizards, enormous rats, spiders—the whole furniture consisting of one huge stone covered with a little straw,

---

[1] The castle of Tours, 147 miles south-west of Paris, which Louis XI. made his favourite residence. See Scott's *Quentin Durward*.—T.

[2] Jean Balue (1471-1491), chaplain to Louis XI. For traitorously divulging the king's schemes to his enemy, the Duke of Burgundy, he was for eleven years shut up in the castle of Loches, in an iron-bound wooden cage.—T.

where the prisoner breathed poison in the very air. . . . Enveloped in the shades of mystery, kept in absolute ignorance of the crime with which he was charged, and the kind of punishment awaiting him, he ceased to belong to the earth!"

If this Bastille of melodrama ever had any existence, the Bastille of the eighteenth century bore the least possible resemblance to it. In 1789, these dungeons on the ground floor of the fortress, with windows looking on the moats, were no longer reserved, as under Louis XV., for prisoners condemned to death, dangerous madmen, or prisoners who had been insolent, obstreperous, or violent; nor for warders guilty of breaches of discipline. At the time of Necker's first ministry, the use of these dungeons had been abolished altogether.

The prisoner, put through an interrogation in the early days of his detention, was never left in ignorance of the "delinquency" with which he was charged, and had no reason to be concerned about the kind of punishment awaiting him; for there had been neither torture nor punishment of any kind at the Bastille for a hundred years.

Instead of a dungeon or a cage of iron, every

prisoner occupied a room of fair size, its greatest defect being that it was rather poorly lighted by a narrow window, secured by bars, some of them projecting inwards. It was sufficiently furnished; and there was nothing to hinder the prisoner from getting in more furniture from outside. Moreover, he could procure whatever clothing and linen he desired, and if he had no means to pay for them, money was supplied. Latude complained of rheumatism, and furs were at once given him. He wanted a dressing-gown of "red-striped calamanco"; the shops were ransacked to gratify him. A certain Hugonnet complained that he had not received the shirts "with embroidered ruffles" which he had asked for. A lady named Sauvé wanted a dress of white silk spotted with green flowers. In all Paris there was only a white dress with green stripes to be found, with which it was hoped that she would be satisfied.

Every room was provided with a fireplace or a stove. Firewood was supplied, and light; the prisoner could have as many candles as he pleased. Paper, pens, and ink were at his disposal; though he was deprived of them temporarily if he made bad

INTRODUCTION

use of them, like Latude, who scribbled all day long only to heap insults in his letters on the governor and the lieutenant of police. He could borrow books from the library, and was at liberty to have books sent in from outside. La Beaumelle had six hundred volumes in his room. He might breed birds, cats, and dogs—by no means being reduced to taming the legendary spider of Pellisson,[1] which figures also in the story of Lauzun,[2] and, indeed, of all prisoners in every age. Instruments of music were allowed. Renneville played the fiddle, and Latude the flute. There were concerts in the prisoners' rooms and in the apartments of the governor.

Every prisoner could work at embroidery, at the turning lathe, or the joiner's bench, at pleasure. All whose conduct was irreproachable were allowed to come and go, to pay each other visits, to play at

[1] A French author (1624-1693) who was involved in the fall of Louis XIV.'s dishonest finance minister, Fouquet, in 1661, and was imprisoned for five years in the Bastille, amusing himself with reading the Fathers of the Church and taming a spider. See Kitchin's *History of France*, iii. 155-157.—T.

[2] Antoine de Caumont, duc de Lauzun (1633-1723), a courtier of Louis XIV., whose favours to the Duke made Louvois, the minister, his bitter enemy. He was twice imprisoned in the Bastille, the second time at the instance of Madame de Montespan. He commanded the French auxiliaries of James II. in Ireland. See Macaulay's *History*, Chaps. IX., XII., XV.—T.

backgammon, cards, or chess in their rooms; at skittles, bowls, or *tonneau*[1] in the courtyard. La Rouèrie asked for a billiard table for himself and his friends, and he got it.

The prisoners were permitted to walk on the platform of the fortress, from which they could see the people passing up and down the Rue Saint-Antoine and the vicinity, and watch the animated crowds on the boulevard at the hours when fashionable people were accustomed to take their drives. By the aid of telescopes and big letters written on boards they were able to communicate with the people of the neighbourhood, and, like Latude, to keep up a secret correspondence with the grisettes of the district. Michelet, with too obvious a design, declares that under Louis XVI. the regulations of the prison were more severe than under Louis XV., and that this promenade on the platform was done away with. There is not a word of truth in it. The promenade was forbidden only to those prisoners who, like the Marquis de Sade, took advantage of it to stir up

[1] A game played with a sort of box, in the top of which are cut holes of equal size, and with metal discs or balls, the object being to pitch the balls into the holes from a distance. A similar game may be seen at any English country fair.—T.

riots among the passers-by; and from the accession of Louis XVI. and the visitation of Malesherbes,[1] the rule of the prison grew milder day by day.

Certain of the prisoners were invited to dine with the governor, and to walk in his gardens, in excellent company. Some were allowed to leave the fortress, on condition of returning in the evening; others were even allowed to remain out all night!

Those who had servants could have them in attendance if the servants were willing to share their captivity. Or they had room-mates, as was the case with Latude and Allègre.

In regard to food, the prisoners are unanimous in declaring that it was abundant and good. "I had five dishes at dinner," says Dumouriez, "and five at supper, without reckoning dessert." The Provost de Beaumont declared that he had quitted the Bastille with regret, because there he had been able to eat and drink to his heart's content. Poultier d'Elmotte says: "M. de Launey had many a friendly

---

[1] The famous president of the Cour des Aides and Minister of the Interior, renowned for his consistent support of the people against oppression. He was banished in 1771 for remonstrating against the abuses of law; but returning to Paris to oppose the execution of Louis XVI., he was guillotined in 1794.—T.

chat with me, and sent me what dishes I wished for." Baron Hennequin, a hypochondriac who found fault with everything, confesses nevertheless that they gave him more meat than he could eat. The Abbé de Buquoy affirms that he fared sumptuously, and that it was the king's intention that the prisoners should be well fed. The splenetic Linguet owns, in his pamphlet, that he had three good meals a day, and that meat was supplied to him in such quantities that his suspicions were aroused: "They meant to poison me!" he says. But he omits to say that de Launey sent him every morning the menu for the day, on which he marked down with his own hand the dishes he fancied, "choosing always the most dainty, and in sufficient quantities to have satisfied five or six epicures."

In Louis XIV.'s time, Renneville drew up the following list of dishes served to him: "Oysters, prawns, fowls, capons, mutton, veal, young pigeons; forcemeat pies and patties; asparagus, cauliflower, green peas, artichokes; salmon, soles, pike, trout, every kind of fish whether fresh-water or salt; pastry, and fruits in their season." We find Latude complaining that the fowls given him were not stuffed!

M. Funck-Brentano tells the amusing story of Marmontel's eating by mistake the dinner intended for his servant, and finding it excellent.

Mdlle. de Launay, afterwards Madame de Staal, who was imprisoned for complicity in the Cellamare [1] plot, relates that on the first evening of her sojourn in the Bastille, she and her maid were both terrified by the strange and prolonged sound, beneath their feet, of a mysterious machine, which conjured up visions of an instrument of torture. When they came to inquire, they found that their room was over the kitchen, and the terrible machine was the roasting-jack!

The prisoners were not only allowed to receive visits from their relations and friends, but to keep them to dinner or to make up a rubber. Thus Madame de Staal held receptions in the afternoon, and in the evening there was high play. "And this time," she says, "was the happiest in my life."

Bussy-Rabutin received the whole court, and all his friends—especially those of the fair sex. M. de Bonrepos—an assumed name—was so comfortable

[1] Antonio del Giudice, prince de Cellamare (1657-1733), the Spanish ambassador, was the instigator of a plot against the Regent in 1718. See Kitchin, *ib*. iii. 474.—T.

in the Bastille that when he was directed to retire to the Invalides,[1] he could only be removed by force.

"I there spent six weeks," says Morellet, "so pleasantly, that I chuckle to this day when I think of them." And when he left, he exclaimed: "God rest those jolly tyrants!"

Voltaire remained there for twelve days, with a recommendation from the lieutenant of police that he should be treated with all the consideration "due to his genius."

The objection may be raised that these cases are all of great lords or men of letters, towards whom the government of those days was exceptionally lenient. (How delightful to find writers put on the same footing with peers!) But the objection is groundless.

I have referred to Renneville and Latude, prisoners of very little account. The one was a spy; the other a swindler. In the three-volume narrative left us by Renneville, you hear of nothing but how he kept open house and made merry with his companions. They gambled and smoked, ate and drank, fuddled and fought, gossiped with their neighbours

---

[1] The Hôtel des Invalides, residence of pensioned soldiers, &c. still a well-known building of Paris.—T.

of both sexes, and passed one another pastry and excellent wine through the chimneys. How gladly the prisoners in our jails to-day would accommodate themselves to such a life! Renneville, assuredly, was not treated with the same consideration as Voltaire; but, frankly, would you have wished it?

As to Latude—who was supplied with dressing-gowns to suit his fancy—the reader will see from M. Funck-Brentano's narrative that no one but himself was to blame if he did not dwell at Vincennes[1] or in the Bastille on the best of terms—or even leave his prison at the shortest notice, by the front gate, and with a well-lined pocket.

For that was one of the harsh measures of this horrible Bastille—to send away the poor wretches, when their time was expired, with a few hundred livres in their pockets, and to compensate such as were found to be innocent! See what M. Funck-Brentano says of Subé, who, for a detention of eighteen days, received 3000 livres (£240 to-day), or of others, who, after an imprisonment of two years, were consoled with an annual pension of 2400 francs

---

[1] A château, four miles east of Paris, notable as the place where St. Louis, the royal lawgiver of France, dispensed justice. The *donjon* still exists, serving now as a soldier's barracks.—T.

of our reckoning. Voltaire spent twelve days in the Bastille, and was assured of an annual pension of 1200 livres for life. What is to be said now of our contemporary justice, which, after some months of imprisonment on suspicion, dismisses the poor fellow, arrested by mistake, with no other indemnity than the friendly admonition: "Go! and take care we don't catch you again!"

Some wag will be sure to say that I am making out the Bastille to have been a palace of delight. We can spare him his little jest. A prison is always a prison, however pleasant it may be; and the best of cheer is no compensation for the loss of liberty. But there is a wide difference, it will be granted, between the reality and the notion generally held—between this "hotel for men of letters," as some one called it, and the hideous black holes of our system of solitary confinement. I once said that I should prefer three years in the Bastille to three months at Mazas.[1] I do not retract.

Linguet and Latude, unquestionably, were the two men whose habit of drawing the long bow has done

[1] One of the first prisons on the system of solitary confinement in cells erected in Paris. It dates from 1850.—T.

most to propagate the fables about the Bastille, the falsity of which is established by incontrovertible documents. Party spirit has not failed to take seriously the interested calumnies of Linguet, who used his spurious martyrdom to advertise himself, and the lies of Latude, exploiting to good purpose a captivity which he had made his career.

Let us leave Linguet, who, after having so earnestly urged the demolition of the Bastille, had reason to regret it at the Conciergerie at the moment of mounting the revolutionary tumbril, and speak a little of the other, this captive who was as ingenious in escaping from prison, when locked up, as in hugging his chains when offered the means of release.

For the bulk of mankind, thirty-five years of captivity was the price Latude paid for a mere practical joke: the sending to Madame de Pompadour of a harmless powder that was taken for poison. The punishment is regarded as terrific: I do not wonder at it. But if, instead of relying on the gentleman's own fanfaronades, the reader will take the trouble to look at the biography written by M. Funck-Brentano and amply supported by documents, he will speedily see that if Latude remained in prison for thirty-five years, it was entirely by his own choice; and that his worst enemy, his most implacable persecutor, the author of all his miseries was—himself.

If, after the piece of trickery which led to his arrest, he had followed the advice of the excellent Berryer, who counselled patience and promised his speedy liberation, he might have got off with a few months of restraint at Vincennes, where his confinement was so rigorous that he had only to push the garden gate to be free!

That was the first folly calculated to injure his cause, for the new fault was more serious than the old. He was caught; he was locked in the cells of the Bastille: but the kind-hearted Berryer soon removed him. Instead of behaving himself quietly, however, our man begins to grow restless, to harangue, to abuse everybody, and on the books lent him to scribble insulting verses on the Pompadour. But they allow him an apartment, then give him a servant, then a companion, Allègre. And then comes the famous escape. One hardly knows which to wonder at the most: the ingenuity of the

INTRODUCTION

two rogues, or the guileless management of this prison which allows them to collect undisturbed a gimlet, a saw, a compass, a pulley, fourteen hundred feet of rope, a rope ladder 180 feet long, with 218 wooden rungs; to conceal all these between the floor and the ceiling below, without anyone ever thinking to look there; and, after having cut through a wall four and a half feet thick, to get clear away without firing a shot!

They were not the first to get across those old walls. Renneville mentions several escapes, the most famous being that of the Abbé de Buquoy.[1] But little importance seems to have been attached to them.

With Allègre and Latude it was a different matter. The passers-by must have seen, in the early morning, the ladder swinging from top to bottom of the wall, and the escape was no longer a secret. The Bastille is discredited. It is possible, then, to escape from

---

[1] The Abbé de Buquoy (1653-1740) owed his imprisonment originally to having been found in company with dealers in contraband salt when the *gabelle*, or salt-tax, compelled the French people to buy salt, whether they wanted it or not, at a price *two thousand times* its true value. He was a man of very eccentric views, one of which was that woman was man's chief evil, and that was why, when the patriarch Job was stripped of children, flocks, herds, &c., his wife was left to him!—T.

it. The chagrined police are on their mettle. There will be laughter at their expense. The fugitives are both well known, too. They will take good care to spread the story of their escape, with plenty of gibes against the governor, the lieutenant of police, the ministry, the favourite, the king! This scandal must be averted at any cost; the fugitives must be caught!

And we cannot help pitying these two wretches who, after a flight so admirably contrived, got arrested so stupidly: Allègre at Brussels, through an abusive letter written to the Pompadour; Latude in Holland, through a letter begging help from his mother.

Latude is again under lock and key, and this time condemned to a stricter confinement. And then the hubbub begins again: outcries, demands, acts of violence, threats! He exasperates and daunts men who had the best will in the world to help him. He is despatched to the fortress of Vincennes, and promised his liberty if he will only keep quiet. His liberation, on his own showing, was but a matter of days. He is allowed to walk on the bank of the moat. He takes advantage of it to escape again!

Captured once more, he is once more lodged at Vincennes, and the whole business begins over again. But they are good enough to consider him a little mad, and after a stay at Charenton,[1] where he was very well treated, he at last gets his dismissal, with the recommendation to betake himself to his own part of the country quietly. Ah, that would not be like Latude! He scampers over Paris, railing against De Sartine, De Marigny; hawking his pamphlets; claiming 150,000 livres as damages!—and, finally, extorting money from a charitable lady by menaces!

This is the last straw. Patience is exhausted, and he is clapped into Bicêtre[2] as a dangerous lunatic. Imagine his fury and disgust!

Let us be just. Suppose, in our own days, a swindler, sentenced to a few months' imprisonment, insulting the police, the magistrates, the court, the president; sentenced on this account to a longer term, escaping once, twice, a third time; always

---

[1] The madhouse, eight miles east of Paris.—T.

[2] A château originally outside Paris, now included in the city itself, once used as a hospital and jail, now a hospital for aged and indigent poor and for lunatics. The first experiments with the guillotine were tried there.—T.

caught, put in jail again, sentenced to still longer terms : then when at last released, after having done his time, scattering broadcast insulting libels against the chief of police, the ministers, the parliament, and insisting on the President of the Republic paying him damages to the tune of 150,000 francs ; to crown it all, getting money out of some good woman by working on her fears ! You will agree with me that such a swaggering blade would not have much difficulty in putting together thirty-five years in jail !

But these sentences would of course be public, and provide no soil for the growth of those legends to which closed doors always give rise. Yet in all that relates to the causes and the duration of the man's imprisonment, his case would be precisely that of Latude—except that for him there would be no furs, no promenading in the gardens, no stuffed fowls for his lunch !

Besides some fifty autograph letters from Latude, addressed from Bicêtre to his good angel, Madame Legros, in which he shows himself in his true character, an intriguing, vain, insolent, bragging, insupportable humbug, I have one, written to M. de Sartine, which Latude published as a pendant to the pamphlet with which he hoped to move Madame de Pompadour to pity, and in which every phrase is an insult. This letter was put up at public auction, and these first lines of it were reproduced in the catalogue:—

"I am supporting with patience the loss of my best years and of my fortune. I am enduring my rheumatism, the weakness of my arm, and a ring of iron around my body for the rest of my life!"

A journalist, one of those who learn their history from Louis Blanc, had a vision of Latude for ever riveted by a ring of iron to a pillar in some underground dungeon, and exclaimed with indignation: "A ring of iron! How horrible!"

And it was only a linen band!

That fabulous iron collar is a type of the whole legend of the unfortunate Latude!

Everything connected with the Bastille has assumed a fabulous character.

What glorious days were those of the 13th and 14th of July, as the popular imagination conjures them up in reliance on Michelet, who, in a vivid, impassioned, picturesque, dramatic, admirable style, has written, not the history, but the romance of the French Revolution!

Look at his account of the 13th. He shows you all Paris in revolt against Versailles, and with superb enthusiasm running to arms to try issues with the royal army. It is fine as literature. Historically, it is pure fiction.

The Parisians were assuredly devoted to the "new ideas," that is, the suppression of the abuses and the privileges specified in the memorials of the States General; in a word, to the reforms longed for by the whole of France. But they had no conception of gaining them without the concurrence of the monarchy, to which they were sincerely attached. That crowd of scared men running to the Hôtel de Ville to demand arms, who are represented by the revolutionary writers as exasperated by the dismissal of Necker and ready to undermine the throne for the sake of that Genevan, were much less alarmed at what was hatching at Versailles than at what was going on in Paris. If they wished for arms, it was for their own security. The dissolution of the National Assembly, which was regarded as certain, was setting all minds in a ferment, and ill-designing people took advantage of the general uneasiness and agitation to drive matters to the worst extremities, creating disorder everywhere. The police had disappeared; the streets were in the hands of the mob. Bands of ruffians—among them those ill-favoured rascals who since the month of May had been flocking, as at a word of command, into Paris from heaven knows where, and who had already been seen at work, pillaging Réveillon's [1] establishment—roamed in every direction, insulting women, stripping wayfarers, looting the shops, opening the prisons, burning the barriers. On July 13 the electors of Paris resolved on the formation of a citizen militia for the protection of the town, and the scheme was adopted on the same day by every district, with articles of constitution, quoted by M. Funck-Brentano, which specify the intentions of the signatories. It was expressly in self-defence against the "Brigands," as they were called, that the citizen militia was formed: "To protect the citizens," ran the minutes of the Petit-Saint-Antoine district, "against the dangers which threaten them each individually." "In a word," says M. Victor Fournel,

[1] See *infra*, p. 83.

"the dominating sentiment was fear. Up till the 14th of July, the Parisian middle-classes showed far more concern at the manifold excesses committed by the populace after Necker's dismissal than at the schemes of the court." And M. Jacques Charavay, who was the first to publish the text of the minutes in question, says not a word too much when he draws from them this conclusion: "The movement which next day swept away the Bastille might possibly have been stifled by the National Guard, if its organization had had greater stability."

All that was wanting to these good intentions was direction, a man at the helm, and particularly the support of Besenval. But his conduct was amazing! He left Versailles with 35,000 men and an order signed by the king—obtained not without difficulty—authorizing him "to repel force by force." Now let us see a summary of his military operations:—

On the 13th, towards four o'clock in the afternoon, a skirmish of the German regiment on the Place Vendôme, where it came into collision with the "demonstration"—as we should say to-day—which was displaying busts of Necker and the Duke of Orleans, and dispersed it.

At six o'clock, a march of the same horse soldiers to the swinging-bridge of the Tuileries, where they had five or six chairs thrown at their head; and the massacre, by M. de Lambesc, of the legendary grey-beard who, an hour after, was describing his tragic end at the Palais-Royal!

At nine o'clock, a military promenade of the same regiment along the boulevards. A volley from the Gardes Françaises slew two of their number, and the regiment beat a retreat without returning fire, to the great surprise of M. de Maleissye, officer of the Guards. For, by his own confession, if the cavalry had charged, it would easily have routed the Gardes Françaises "in the state of drunkenness in which they then were."

And Besenval, terrified at such a resistance, assembled all his troops, shut himself up with them in the Champ de Mars, and did not move another step!

We ask ourselves, "Was he a fool? or was he a traitor?" He was a fool, for he thought he had "three hundred thousand men" in front of him, took every excited person for a rebel, and did not understand that out of every hundred Parisians there were ninety who were relying on him to bring the mutineers to reason.

He had no confidence in his troops, he said.

It was rather for them to have no confidence in him, and to lose heart utterly at such a spectacle of cowardice. But he was slandering them. One solitary regiment showed disloyalty. And if he had only given the Swiss the word to march, their conduct on August 10 gives ample proof that they could have been depended on.

"And then," says he again, "I was fearful of letting loose civil war!"

Indeed! And so a soldier going to suppress a revolt is not to run the risk of fighting!

Last reason of all: "I requested orders from Versailles—and did not get them!"

What, then, had he in his pocket?

Finally, after having sent word to Flesselles and De Launey to maintain their position till he arrived, and after having allowed the arms of the Invalides to be looted under his eyes without a single effort to save them, he waited till the Bastille was taken before making up his mind to leave the Champ de Mars, and to return quietly to

Versailles with his 35,000 men, who had not fired a shot!

Ah! those were the days for rioting!

"On July 13," says Michelet, "Paris was defending herself." (Against whom?) "On the 14th, she attacked! A voice wakened her and cried, 'On, and take the Bastille!' And that day was the day of the entire People!"

Admirable poetry; but every word a lie!

Listen to Marat, who is not open to suspicion, and who saw things at closer quarters. "The Bastille, badly defended, was captured by a handful of soldiers and a gang of wretches for the most part Germans and provincials. The Parisians, those everlasting star-gazers, came there out of curiosity!"

In reality, Michelet's "entire people" reduces itself to a bare thousand assailants, of whom three hundred at most took part in the fight: Gardes Françaises and deserters of all arms, lawyers' clerks, and citizens who had lost their heads: fine fellows who thought themselves engaged in meritorious work in rushing on these inoffensive walls; bandits attracted by the riot which promised them theft and murder with impunity. And a number of mere spectators—spectators above all!

"I was present," says Chancellor Pasquier, "at the taking of the Bastille. What is called the fight was not serious. The resistance was absolutely nil. The truth is, that this grand fight did not cause an instant's alarm to the spectators, who had flocked up to see the result. Among them there were many ladies of the greatest elegance. In order to get more easily to the front they had left their carriages at a distance. By my side was Mdlle. Contat, of the Comédie Française. We stayed to see the finish, and then I escorted her on my arm to her carriage in the Place Royale."

"The Bastille was not taken; truth must be told, it surrendered." It is Michelet himself who makes this statement, and he adds: "what ruined it was its own evil conscience!"

It would be too simple to acknowledge that it was the incapacity of its governor.

There is no connoisseur in old prints but is acquainted with those last-century views which represent the taking of the Bastille. The platform of the fortress bristles with cannon all firing together, "belching forth death,"—without the slightest attention on the part of the assailants, for all the balls from this artillery, passing over their heads, would only kill inoffensive wayfarers without so much as scratching a single one of the besiegers! And the Bastille did not fire a single shot in self-defence!

In the morning, at the request of Thuriot de la Rozière, De Launey had readily consented to the withdrawal of the fifteen cannon of the platform from their embrasures, and had blocked up the embrasures with planks. Of the three guns which later on he ranged batterywise before the entrance gate, not one was effective, and the discharge attributed to one of them came from a piece of ordnance on the wall.

He placed such absolute reliance on succour from Besenval that, on evacuating the arsenal and getting the whole garrison together into the Bastille —eighty-two Invalides and M. de Flue's thirty-two Swiss—he had forgotten to increase his stock of provisions. Now, the Bastille had no reserve of provisions. Every morning, like a good housewife, it received the goods ordered the night before, brought by the different purveyors; on this day, they were intercepted. So it happened that at three o'clock in the afternoon the garrison was without its usual rations, and the Invalides, who had been for a week past going in and out of all the inns in the neighbourhood, and were disposed to open the doors to their good friends of the suburbs, used the scantiness of their rations as a pretext for mutiny, for refusing to fight, and for muddling the brains, never very clear, of the unhappy De Launey.

"On the day of my arrival," says De Flue, "I was able to take this man's measure from the absolutely imbecile preparations which he made for the defence of his position. I saw clearly that we should be very poorly led in case of attack. He was so struck with terror at the idea of it that, when night came on, he took the shadows of trees for enemies! Incapable, irresolute, devoting all his attention to trifles and neglecting important duties—such was the man."

Abandoned by Besenval, instead of cowing his Invalides into obedience by his energy, and maintaining his position to famishing point behind walls over which the balls of the besiegers flew without killing more than one man, De Launey lost his head, made a feint of firing the powder magazine, capitulated, and opened his gates to men who, as Chateaubriand says, " could never have cleared them if he had only kept them shut."

If this poor creature had done his duty, and Besenval had done his, things would have had quite a different complexion. That is not to say that the Revolution would have been averted—far from it! The Revolution was legitimate, desirable, and, under the generous impulse of a whole nation, irresistible. But it would have followed another bent, and would have triumphed at a slighter cost, with less ruin and less bloodshed. The consequences of the 14th of July were disastrous. The mere words, "The Bastille is taken!" were the signal for the most frightful disorders throughout France. It seemed as though those old walls were dragging down with them in their fall all authority, all respect, all discipline; as though the floodgates were being opened to every kind of excess. Peasants went about in bands, ravaging, pillaging, firing the châteaux, the burghers' houses, and burning alive those who fell into their hands. The soldiers mutinied, insulted their chiefs, and fell to carousing with the malefactors whom they set free. There was not a town or village where the mob did not put on menacing airs, where decent people were not molested by the brawlers of the clubs and the street-corners. Such violence led to a rapid reaction, and there were numerous defections—of men who, on the very eve of the outbreak, among the magistracy, the army, the clergy, the nobility, though sympathizing with the new ideas, abruptly cut themselves loose from the movement, like the good Duke de la Rochefoucauld, who exclaimed, "Liberty is not entered by such a door as this!" Hovering between the desire and the fear of granting the promised reforms, urged on one side to resistance, on the other to submission, and more than ever destitute of all political acumen and all will power, the king went to Paris, and, bending before the revolt, approved of the assassination of his most faithful servants—and took, on that fatal day, his first step towards the scaffold! Henceforth, under the pressure of the populace, to whom its first success had shown the measure of its strength, and who became every day more exacting, more threatening, the Revolution was to go on in its perverse course, stumbling at every step, until it came to the orgy of '93, which, properly speaking, was only the systematizing of brigandage. Malouet was right indeed: what we symbolize in our festival of the 14th of July is not the rising sun, the dawn of Liberty; it is the first lurid lightning flash of the Terror!

Doctor Rigby, after having walked up and down the whole afternoon in the Jardin Monceau without the least idea of what was going on in the Suburb Saint-Antoine, returned in the evening to his house near the Palais-Royal. He saw the mob reeling in drunkenness. Men and women were laughing, crying, and embracing one another: "The Bastille is taken! At last we are free!" And not the least enthusiastic were those very men of the citizen militia who, ready yesterday to fight the insurrection, were to-day hailing its triumph! The first sabre brandished by the first national guard was in point of fact that of Joseph Prudhomme![1]

[1] The title rôle in a comedy by Henri Mounier, entitled *Grandeur et décadence de M. Joseph Prudhomme* (1852). He is a writing-master, very vain, given (like Mr. Micawber) to tall talk and long-winded periods.

All at once this delirious crowd shudders, parts asunder with cries of horror!

Down the Rue Saint-Honoré comes a yelling mob of wine-soaked malefactors, bearing along, at the ends of two pikes, the still bleeding heads of De Launey and De Flesselles!

And the silly folk, so madly rejoiced by the fall of an imaginary tyranny which has not even the wits to defend itself, go their several ways, struck dumb with consternation.

For here the Real is making its entrance!

Do not fancy that because the Bastille has opened its gates, the legends which give it so cruel a name are going to vanish into thin air, like the phantoms of an ancient château when light is let in.

While Michelet's "entire Paris" is making short work of the Invalides who surrendered the place; cutting in pieces the man who prevented its blowing up; slaughtering Major de Losme, the friend and

He has become typical of "much cry and little wool." As an officer of the National Guard he says, "This sabre constitutes the finest day in my life! I accept it, and if ever I find myself at the head of your phalanxes, I shall know how to use it in defence of our institutions— and, if need arise, to fight for them!"—T.

benefactor of the prisoners; torturing the hapless De Launey, who, from the Bastille to the Hôtel de Ville, stabbed, slashed, hacked with sabres and pikes and bayonets, is finally decapitated by the aid of a short knife—an episode which Michelet skilfully slurs over—while all the criminals of the district, crowding along in the wake of the combatants, are rushing to the official buildings, looting, smashing, throwing into the moats furniture, books, official papers, archives, the remnants of which will be collected with such difficulty—some good people are saying to themselves: "But come now, there are some prisoners! Suppose we go and set them free?"

Here let us see what Louis Blanc has to say:—

"Meanwhile the doors of the cells" (he insists on the cells) "were burst in with a mighty effort; the prisoners were free! Alas! for three of them it was too late! The first, whose name was the Comte de Solages, a victim for seven years of the incomprehensible vengeance of an implacable father, found neither relatives who would consent to acknowledge him, nor his property, which had become the prey of covetous collateral heirs! The second was called Whyte. Of what crime was he guilty, accused, of, at any rate, suspected? No one has ever known! The man himself was questioned in vain. In the Bastille he had lost his reason. The third, Tavernier, at the sight of his deliverers, fancied he saw his executioners coming, and put himself on the defensive. Throwing their arms round his neck they undeceived him; but next day he was met roaming through the town, muttering wild and whirling words. He was mad!"

As many wilful errors as there are words!

The Comte de Solages was an execrable libertine, confined at the request of his family for "atrocious and notorious crimes." His relatives nevertheless had the humanity to take him in after his deliverance, and it was with them that he died in 1825.

Whyte and Tavernier did not go mad in the Bastille. They were in the Bastille because they were mad; and the second was, further, implicated in an assassination. Finding shelter with a perruquier of the neighbourhood, he set about smashing all his host's belongings, which necessitated his banishment to Charenton, where Whyte soon rejoined him. It was not worth the trouble of changing their quarters!

Introduction

Four other prisoners who were set free, Corrège, Bechade, Pujade, and Laroche, were imprisoned for forgery. And so Louis Blanc is careful silently to pass them over!

Ten days before, another victim of tyranny had been groaning in irons—the Marquis de Sade, who, from the height of the platform, used to provoke the passers-by with the aid of a speaking trumpet. De Launey was compelled to transfer him to Vincennes, thus depriving the victors of the glory of liberating the future author of *Justine*. The Republic took its revenge in making him later secretary of the "Pike" ward,[1] an office for which he was marked out by his virtues!

But of all these prisoners the most celebrated, the most popular, the man whose misfortunes all Paris deplored, was the famous Comte de Lorges, who, according to the biographical sketch devoted to him by the unknown author of his deliverance, had been shut up for thirty-two years. The story must be read in the pamphlet of Citizen Rousselet, conqueror of the Bastille: "The tide of humanity penetrates into

---

[1] In the early days of the Revolution, Paris was divided into sections or wards, and as the *pike* had played a great part in the recent disturbances, one of the wards was known as the "Pike" section.—T.

ways narrowed by mistrust. An iron door opens: what does one see? Is this a man? Good heavens! this old man loaded with irons! the splendour of his brow, the whiteness of his beard hanging over his breast! What majesty! the fire still flashing from his eyes seems to shed a gentle light in this lugubrious abode!"

Surprised at seeing so many armed men, he asks them if Louis XV. is still alive. They set him free, they lead him to the Hôtel de Ville.

For fifteen days all Paris went to visit the black dungeon in which this unhappy wretch had been shut up for so many years without other light than that which escaped "from his eyes"! A stone from that dungeon had a place in the Curtius Museum. His portrait was published. A print represents him at the moment when his chains were broken, seated on a chair in his cell, a pitcher of water by his side!

And this hapless greybeard—he was never seen! He never existed!

In reality there were in the Bastille, on the 14th of July, only seven prisoners—two madmen, a *Sadique*,[1]

[1] A disciple of the Marquis de Sade (see p. 35), a notorious debauchee, whose book *Justine* was a disgusting mixture of brutality and obscenity.—T.

and four forgers. But about their number and their right to imprisonment Michelet remains dumb: to discuss that would spoil his epic! And he excels in making the most of everything that can support his case, and in ignoring everything that damages it. And so he contents himself with speaking of the two who had "gone mad"!—a prevarication worthy of Louis Blanc, nay, unworthy even of him!

The conquerors were somewhat surprised at the small number of victims, more surprised still to find them comfortably installed in rooms, some of which were furnished with arm-chairs in Utrecht velvet! The author of *The Bastille Unmasked* exclaims: "What! No corpses! No skeletons! No men in chains!" "The taking of the Bastille," said "Cousin Jacques,"[1] "has opened the eyes of the public on the kind of captivity experienced there."

But in this he was greatly mistaken. Legends die hard! A Bastille without cells, dungeons, cages of iron! Public opinion did not admit that it could have been deceived on that point.

"Several prisoners," says the *History of Remark-*

---

[1] The pseudonym of Beffroy de Reigny (1757-1811), author of farces, and of a *Précis historique de la prise de la Bastille*.—T.

able Events, "were set at liberty; but some, and perhaps the greater number, had already died of hunger, because men could not find their way about this monstrous prison. Some of these prisoners confined within four walls received food only through holes cut in the wall. A party of prisoners was found starved to death, because their cells were not discovered till several days had elapsed!"

Another pamphlet on the underground cells discovered in the Bastille, resuscitating an old fable which had already done duty for the Cardinal de Richelieu, shows us a prisoner taken from his cell and led by the governor into "a room which had nothing sinister in its appearance. It was lit by more than fifty candles. Sweet-scented flowers filled it with a delicious perfume. The tyrant chatted amicably with his prisoner. . . . Then he gave the horrible signal: a bascule let into the floor opened, and the wretched man disappeared, falling upon a wheel stuck with razors and set in motion by invisible hands." And the author winds up with this magnificent reflection:—" Such a punishment, so basely contrived, is not even credible—and yet it was at Paris, in that beautiful and flourishing city, that this took place!"

Dorat-Cubières, who was one of the literary disgraces of the eighteenth century, goes further! He saw, with his own eyes, one of those dens where the captive, shut up with enough bread to last him a week, had thereafter nothing else to subsist on but his own flesh. "In this den," he says, "we came upon a horrible skeleton, the sight of which made me shrink back with horror!"

And the popular picture-mongers did not fail to propagate these insanities. I have an engraving of the time nicely calculated to stir sensitive hearts. Upon the steps of a gloomy cellar the conquerors are dragging along a man whom his uniform shows to be one of the defenders of the Bastille, and are pointing out to him an old man being carried away, another being cut down from the ceiling where he is hanging by the arms; yet others lying on a wheel furnished with iron teeth, chained to it, twisted into horrible contortions by abominable machines; and in a recess behind a grating appears the skeleton—which Dorat-Cubières never saw!

The non-existence of these dungeons and holes

with skeletons was too great a shock to settled beliefs. This Bastille *must* contain concealed below ground some unknown cells where its victims were moaning! And naturally enough, when one bent down the ear, one heard their despairing appeals! But after having pierced through vaults, sunk pits, dug, sounded everywhere, there was no help for it but to give up these fancies, though—an agreeable thing to have to say!—with regret.

They fell back then on instruments of torture. For though the rack had been abolished for a hundred years, how was it possible to conceive of the Bastille without some slight instruments of torture?

They had no difficulty in finding them—"chains," says Louis Blanc, "which the hands of many innocent men had perhaps worn, machines of which no one could guess the use: an old iron corslet which seemed to have been invented to reduce man to everlasting immobility!"

As a matter of fact, these chains belonged to two statuettes of prisoners which stood on either side of the great clock in the courtyard. The machines, the use of which no one could guess, were the fragments of a clandestine printing-press that had been pulled to pieces. And the iron corslet was a piece of fifteenth-century armour!

Skeletons, too, were missing, though indeed some bones were found in the apartment of the surgeon of the fortress; but the utmost bad faith could not but be compelled to acknowledge that these were anatomical specimens. Happily for the legend, a more serious discovery was made: "two skeletons, chained to a cannon-ball," as the register of the district of Saint-Louis la Culture declared.

They both came to light in the rubbish dug out during the construction of the bastion afterwards turned into a garden for the governor. "One," says the report of Fourcroy, Vicq-d'Azyr, and Sabatier, instructed to examine them, "was found turned head downwards on the steps of a steep staircase, entirely covered with earth, and appears to be that of a workman who had fallen by accident down this dark staircase, where he was not seen by the men working at the embankment. The other, carefully buried in a sort of ditch, had evidently been laid there a long time previously, before there was any idea of filling up the bastion."

As to the cannon-ball, it must have dated back to the Fronde.[1]

But skeletons were necessary! They had found some: they might as well profit by them!

The demolisher of the Bastille, that charlatan Palloy, exhibited them to the veneration of the faithful in a cellar by the light of a funereal lamp, after which they were honoured with a magnificent funeral, with drums, clergy, a procession of working men, between two lines of National Guards, from the Bastille to the Church of St. Paul. And finally, in the graveyard adjoining the church, they raised to them, amid four poplars, a monument of which a contemporary print has preserved the likeness.

After such a ceremony, dispute if you dare the authenticity of the relics!

The memory of the Man in the Iron Mask is so closely bound up with the story of the Bastille that M.

---

[1] The name given to the constitutional struggles of the nobles and the Parlement of Paris against Mazarin and the royal power (1648-1654). The name is derived from *fronde*, a sling. A wit of the Parlement, one Bachaumont, "told the lawyers of that august body that they were like schoolboys playing in the town ditches with their slings, who run away directly the watchman appears, and begin again when his back is turned." See Kitchin, iii. pp. 102-128.—T.

Introduction

Funck-Brentano could not neglect this great enigma about which for two hundred years so much ink has been spilt. He strips off this famous mask—which, by the way, was of velvet—and shows us the face which the world has been so anxious to see: the face of Mattioli, the confidant of the Duke of Mantua and the betrayer of both Louis XIV. and his own master.

M. Funck-Brentano's demonstration is so convincing as to leave no room for doubt. But one dare not hope that the good public will accept his conclusions as final. To the public, mystery is ever more attractive than the truth. There is a want of prestige about Mattioli; while about a twin brother of Louis XIV.—ah, *there* is something that appeals to the imagination!

And then there are the guides, the showmen, to reckon with—those faithful guardians of legends, whose propaganda is more aggressive than that of scholars. When you reflect that every day, at the Isles of Saint-Marguerite, the masked man's cell is shown to visitors by a good woman who retails all the traditional fables about the luxurious life of the prisoner, his lace, his plate, and the attentions shown him by M. de Saint-Mars, you will agree that a struggle with this daily discourse would be hopeless. And you would not come off with a whole skin!

I was visiting the Château d'If before the new buildings were erected. The show-woman of the place, another worthy dame, pointed out to us the ruined cells of the Abbé Faria and Edmond Dantès.[1] And the spectators were musing on the story as they contemplated the ruins.

"It seems to me," I said, "that these cells are rather near one another, but surely Alexandre Dumas put them a little farther apart!"

"Oh, well!" replied the good creature, withering me with a glance of contempt, "if, when I'm relating gospel truth, the gentleman begins quoting a novelist—!"

To come nearer home. Follow, one of these days, a batch of Cook's tourists at Versailles, shown round by an English cicerone. You will see him point out the window from which Louis XVI. issued, on a flying bridge, to reach his scaffold, erected in the marble court! The guide is no fool. He knows well enough that the Place de la Concorde would

[1] See *Monte-Cristo*.—T.

not appeal to the imagination of his countrymen; while it is quite natural to them to draw a parallel in their minds between the scaffold of Louis XVI. at Versailles and that of Charles I. at Whitehall.

And the conclusion of the whole matter is this: that whatever may be said or written, nothing will prevail against the popular beliefs that the Bastille was "the hell of living men," and that it was taken by storm. Legends are the history of the people, especially those which flatter their instincts, prejudices, and passions. You will never convince them of their falsity.

M. Funck-Brentano must also expect to be treated as a "reactionary," for such is, to many people, any one who does not unreservedly decry the *ancien régime*. It had, assuredly, its vices and abuses, which the Revolution swept away—to replace them by others, much more tolerable, to be sure; but that is no reason for slandering the past and painting it blacker than it really was. The fanatical supporters of the Revolution have founded in its honour a sort of cult whose intolerance is often irritating. To hear them you would fancy that before its birth there was nothing but darkness, ignorance, iniquity, and wretchedness! And so we are to give it wholehearted admiration, and palliate its errors and its crimes; even gilding, as Chateaubriand said, the iron of its guillotine. These idolaters of the Revolution are very injudicious. By endeavouring to compel admiration for all that it effected, good and ill without distinction, they provoke the very unreasonable inclination to regard its whole achievement with abhorrence. It could well dispense with such a surplusage of zeal, for it is strong enough to bear the truth; and its work, after all, is great enough to need no justification or glorification by means of legends.

VICTORIEN SARDOU.

LEGENDS OF THE BASTILLE

CHAPTER I.

THE ARCHIVES.

"THE Bastille," wrote Sainte-Foix, "is a castle which, without being strong, is one of the most formidable in Europe, and about it I shall say nothing." "Silence is safer than speech on that subject," was the saying in Paris.

At the extremity of the Rue Saint-Antoine, as one entered the suburb, appeared the eight lofty towers, sombre, massive, plunging their moss-grown feet into pools of muddy water. Their walls were pierced at intervals with narrow, iron-barred windows: they were crowned with battlements. Situated not far from the Marais, the blithe and wealthy quarter, and quite near to the Suburb Saint-Antoine, where industry raised its perpetual hum, the Bastille, charged with gloom and silence, formed an impressive contrast.

The common impression it made is conveyed by Restif

de la Bretonne in his *Nights of Paris* : "It was a nightmare, that awesome Bastille, on which, as I passed each evening along the Rue Saint-Gilles, I never dared to turn my eyes."

The towers had an air of mystery, harsh and melancholy, and the royal government threw mystery like a cloud around them. At nightfall, when the shutters were closed, a cab would cross the drawbridge, and from time to time, in the blackness of night, funeral processions, vague shadows which the light of a torch set flickering on the walls, would make their silent exit. How many of those who had entered there had ever been seen again? And if perchance one met a former prisoner, to the first question he would reply that on leaving he had signed a promise to reveal nothing of what he had seen. This former prisoner had, as a matter of fact, never seen anything to speak of. Absolute silence was imposed upon the warders. "There is no exchanging of confidences in this place," writes Madame de Staal, "and the people you come across have all such freezing physiognomies that you would think twice before asking the most trifling question." "The first article of their code," says Linguet, "is the impenetrable mystery which envelops all their operations."

We know how legends are formed. Sometimes you see them open out like flowers brilliant under the sun's bright beams, you see them blossom under the glorious radiance that lights up the life of heroes. The man himself has long gone down into the tomb; the legend survives; it streams across the ages, like a meteor leaving its trail of light; it grows, broadens out, with ever-increasing lustre and glow: in this light we see Themistocles, Leonidas, Alexander, Cæsar, Charlemagne, Napoleon.

Or may be, on the contrary, the legend is born in some remote corner, covered with shade and silence. There men have lived their lives, there it has been their lot to suffer. Their moans have risen in solitude and confinement, and the only ears that heard them were harder than their stone walls. These moans, heard by no compassionate soul, the great resounding soul of the people catches up, swelling them with all its might. Soon, among the mass of the people, there passes a blast irresistible in its strength, like the tempest that upheaves the restless waves. Then is the sea loosed from its chains: the tumultuous breakers dash upon the affrighted shore: the sea-walls are all swept away!

In a letter written by Chevalier, the major of the Bastille, to Sartine, the chief of the police, he spoke of the common gossip on the Bastille that was going about. "Although utterly false," he said, "I think it very dangerous on account of its dissemination through the kingdom, and that has now been going on for several years." No attention was paid to Chevalier's warning. Mystery continued to be the rule at the Bastille and in all that related to it. "The mildness of manners and of the government," writes La Harpe, "had caused needlessly harsh measures in great part to disappear. They lived on in the imagination of the people, augmented and strengthened by the tales which credulity and hate seize upon." Ere long the *Memoirs* of Latude and of Linguet appeared. Latude concealed his grievous faults, to paint his long sufferings in strokes of fire. Linguet, with his rare literary talent, made of the Bastille a picture dark in the extreme, compressing the gist of his pamphlet into the sentence : "Except perhaps in hell, there are no tortures to approach those of the Bastille." At the same period, the great Mirabeau was launching his powerful plea against *lettres de cachet*, "arbitrary orders." These books produced a mighty reverberation. The Revolution broke out like a clap of thunder. The Bastille was disembowelled. The frowning towers crumbled stone by stone under the picks of the demolishers, and, as if they had been the pedestal of the *ancien régime*, that too toppled over with a crash.

One of the halls of the Bastille contained, in boxes carefully arranged, the entire history of the celebrated fortress from the year 1659, at which date the foundation of this precious store of archives had been begun. There were collected the documents concerning, not only the prisoners of the Bastille, but all the persons who had been lodged there, either under sentence of exile, or simply arrested within the limits of the generality of Paris in virtue of a *lettre de cachet*.

The documents in this store-room had been in charge of archivists, who throughout the eighteenth century had laboured with zeal and intelligence at putting in order papers which, on the eve of the Revolution, were counted by hundreds of thousands. The whole mass was now in perfect order, classified and docketed. The major of the château, Chevalier, had even been commissioned to make these documents the basis of a history of the prisoners.

The Bastille was taken. In the disorder, what was the fate of the archives? The ransacking of the papers continued for two days, writes Dusaulx, one of the commissioners elected by the Assembly for the preservation of the archives of the Bastille. "When, on Thursday the 16th, my colleagues and myself went down into the sort of cellar where the archives were, we found the boxes in very orderly arrangement on the shelves, but they were already empty. The most important documents had been carried off: the rest were strewn on the floor, scattered about the courtyard, and even in the moats. However, the curious still found some gleanings there." The testimony of Dusaulx is only too well confirmed. "I went to see the siege of the Bastille," writes Restif de la Bretonne; "when I arrived it was all over, the place was taken. Infuriated men were throwing papers, documents of great historical value, from the top of the towers into the moats." Among these papers, some had been burnt, some torn, registers had been torn to shreds and trailed in the mud. The mob had invaded the halls of the château: men of learning and mere curiosity hunters strove eagerly to get possession of as many of these documents as possible, in which they thought they were sure to find startling revelations. "There is talk of the son of a celebrated magistrate," writes Gabriel Brizard, "who went off with his carriage full of them." Villenave, then twenty-seven years of age and already a collector, gathered a rich harvest for his study, and Beaumarchais, in the course of a patriotic ramble through the interior of the captured fortress, was careful to get together a certain number of these papers.

The papers purloined from the archives on the day of the capture and the day following became dispersed throughout France and Europe. A large packet came into the hands of Pierre Lubrowski, an attaché in the Russian embassy. Sold in 1805, with his whole collection, to the Emperor Alexander, the papers were deposited in the Hermitage Palace. To-day they are preserved in the Imperial Library at St. Petersburg.

Fortunately, the custody of the captured fortress was entrusted on July 15 to the company of arquebusiers, which received orders to prevent the removal of any more papers. On July 16 one of the members present at a sitting of the Electoral Assembly, sprang forward to the table and cried, " Ah, gentlemen, let us save the papers! It is said that the papers of the Bastille are being plundered; let us hasten to collect the remnants of these old title-deeds of an intolerable despotism, so that we may inspire our latest posterity with their horror!" There was rapturous applause. A committee was nominated, consisting of Dusaulx, De Chamseru,

Gorneau, and Cailleau. Let us follow the style of the period : " Before the Bastille the commissioners received a triumphant reception. Amid the cheers of the people, who had been informed of their mission, ten distinguished men of letters besought them to lead the commissioners into the heart of that famous fortress, so long detested." When they got into the Bastille, the commissioners were not long in perceiving that they were a little behind the fair : " Many boxes were empty, and there was an immense heap of papers in complete disorder."

The question of the papers of the Bastille grew day by day extraordinarily popular. The Electoral Assembly had just appointed commissioners to collect them ; La Fayette, commander of the National Guards, imposed a similar duty on the St. Elizabeth district ; Bailly, the mayor of Paris, delegated Dusaulx to the same office. In the Constituent Assembly, the Comte de Châtenay-Lanty proposed that the municipality of Paris should be instructed to get together the papers found at the Bastille, so that they might be arranged, and that extracts from them might be printed and published, "in order to keep for ever alive in the hearts of Frenchmen, by means of this reading, the detestation of arbitrary orders and the love of liberty"! This book was to be the preface to the constitution. Finally, the district of St. Roch took the initiative in calling upon the electors to restore to the nation the papers carried off from the Bastille by Beaumarchais.

In the sitting of July 24, the Electoral Assembly

passed a resolution enjoining such citizens as were in possession of papers from the Bastille to bring them back to the Hôtel de Ville. The appeal was responded to, and the restitutions were numerous.

When the pillage and destruction had been stopped and possession had been regained of a part of the stolen documents, the papers were consigned to three different depositories; but it was not long before they were deposited all together in the convent of St. Louis la Culture. At length, on November 2, 1791, the Commune of Paris resolved to have the precious documents placed in the city library. The decision was so much the more happy in that the transfer, while placing the papers under the guardianship of trained men and genuine librarians, did not necessitate removal, since the city library at that date occupied the same quarters as the archives of the Bastille, namely, the convent of St. Louis la Culture.

To the revolutionary period succeeded times of greater calm. The archives of the Bastille, after being the object of so much discussion, and having occupied the Constituent Assembly, the Electoral Assembly, the Paris Commune, the press, Mirabeau, La Fayette, Bailly, all Paris, the whole of France, fell into absolute oblivion. They were lost from sight; the very recollection of them was effaced. In 1840, a young librarian named François Ravaisson discovered them in the Arsenal library at the bottom of a veritable dungeon. How had they got stranded there?

Ameilhon, the city librarian, had been elected on April 22, 1797, keeper of the Arsenal library. Anxious to enrich the new depository of which he had become the head, he obtained a decree handing over the papers of the Bastille to the Arsenal library. The librarians recoiled in dismay before this invasion of documents, more than 600,000 in number and in the most admired disorder. Then, having put their heads together, they had the papers crammed into a dusty back-room, putting off the sorting of them from day to day. Forty years slipped away. And if it happened that some old antiquary, curious and importunate, asked to be allowed to consult the documents he had heard spoken of in his youth, he was answered—no doubt in perfect good faith—that they did not know what he was talking about.

In 1840 François Ravaisson had to get some repairs done in his kitchen at the Arsenal library. The slabs of the flooring were raised, when there came to view, in the yawning hole, a mass of old papers. It happened by the merest chance that, as he drew a leaf out of the heap, Ravaisson laid his hand on a *lettre de cachet*. He understood at once that he had just discovered the lost treasure. Fifty years of laborious effort have now restored the order which the victors of the 14th of July and successive removals had destroyed. The archives of the Bastille still constitute, at the present day, an imposing collection, in spite of the gaps made by fire and pillage in 1789, for ever to be regretted. The administration of the Arsenal library has acquired copies of the documents coming from the Bastille which are preserved at St. Petersburg. The archives of the Bastille are now open to inspection by any visitor to the Arsenal library, in rooms specially fitted up for them. Several registers had holes burnt in them on the day of the capture of the Bastille, their binding is scorched black, their leaves are yellow. In the boxes the documents are now numbered, and they are daily consulted by men of letters. The catalogue has been compiled and published recently, through the assiduity of the minister of public instruction.

It is by the light of these documents, of undeniable genuineness and authority, that the black shade which so long brooded over the Bastille has at length been dispelled. The legends have melted away in the clear light of history, as the thick cloak of mist with which night covers the earth is dissipated by the morning sun; and enigmas which mankind, wearied of fruitless investigations, had resigned itself to declare insoluble, have now at last been solved.

CHAPTER II.

HISTORY OF THE BASTILLE.

JULIUS CÆSAR describes a structure three stories high which his legionaries used rapidly to erect in front of towns they were besieging. Such was the remote origin of the "bastides" or "bastilles," as these movable fortresses were called in the Middle Ages. Froissart, speaking of a place that was being invested, says that "bastides were stationed on the roads and in the open country" in such a manner that the town could get no food supplies. It was not long before the designation was applied to the fixed towers erected on the ramparts for the defence of the towns, and more particularly to those which were constructed at the entrance gates.

In 1356, the chroniclers mention some important works that had been done on the circumvallations of Paris. These were constructions interrupting the wall at intervals, and so placed as to protect either an entrance gate or the wall itself. The special designations of *eschiffles*, *guérites*, or *barbacanes* were applied to such of these buildings as rose between two gates of the city, while the *bastilles* or *bastides* were those which defended the gates. The first stone of the edifice which for more than four centuries was to remain famous under the name of the Bastille was laid on April 22, 1370, by the mayor of Paris in person, Hugh Aubriot, the object being to strengthen the defences of the city against the English. To reproach the king, Charles V., with the construction of a cruel prison would be almost as reasonable as to reproach Louis-Philippe with the construction of the fortress of Mont Valérien. We borrow these details from M. Fernand Bournon's excellent work on the Bastille in the *Histoire générale de Paris*.

"The Bastille," writes M. Bournon, "at the time of its capture on July 14, 1789, was still identical, except in some trifling particulars, with the work of the architects of the fourteenth century." The Place de la Bastille of the present day does not correspond exactly to the site of the fortress. Mentally to restore that site it is necessary to take away the last houses of the Rue Saint-Antoine and the Boulevard Henri IV.; the ground they occupy was then covered with the château and its glacis. The round towers, however, must have extended considerably in advance of the line of the houses and have encroached upon the pavement. The plan reproducing the site exactly is to-day marked by lines of white stones, by means of which all Parisians may get some notion of it if they go to the Place de la Bastille.

M. Augé de Lassus, who drew so largely upon the works of M. Bournon and ourselves for his lecture on the

Bastille,[1] will permit us in our turn to borrow from him the description he gave of the Bastille, so far as its construction is concerned. Prints of the commonest kind which have circulated in thousands, the more recent reconstruction which in 1889 gave Paris so much entertainment, have familiarized us with the aspect of the Bastille, whose eight circular towers, connected by curtains of equal height, give us the impression of a box all of a piece, or, if you prefer it, an enormous sarcophagus. The eight towers all had their names. There were the Corner, the Chapel, and the Well towers, names readily accounted for by their position or by details of their construction. Then came the Bertaudière and Bazinière towers, baptized by the names of two former prisoners. The Treasure tower was so called because it had received on many occasions, notably under Henri IV., the custody of the public money. The excellent poet Mathurin Regnier alludes to this fact in these oft-quoted lines:—

> "Now mark these parsons, sons of ill-got gain,
> Whose grasping sires for years have stolen amain,
> Whose family coffers vaster wealth conceal,
> Than fills that royal store-house, the Bastille."

The seventh tower was known as the County tower, owing its name, as M. Bournon conjectures, to the feudal dignity called the County of Paris. "The hypothesis," he adds, "derives the greater weight from the fact that the mayors of Paris were called, up to the end of the

[1] Delivered to the French Association for the Advancement of Science in 1893.

ancien régime, mayors of the town and viscounty of Paris."
The eighth tower bore a name which, for the tower of a prison, is very remarkable. It was called the Tower of Liberty. This odd appellation had come to it from the circumstance that it had been the part of the Bastille where prisoners were lodged who enjoyed exceptionally favourable treatment, those who had the "liberty" of walking during the day in the courtyards of the château. These prisoners were said to be "in the liberty of the court"; the officers of the château called them the "prisoners of the liberty" in contradistinction to the prisoners "in durance"; and that one of the eight towers in which they were lodged was thus, quite naturally, called "the Tower of Liberty."

The towers of the Chapel and the Treasure, which were the oldest, had flanked the original gateway, but this was soon walled up, leaving however in the masonry the outline of its arch, and even the statues of saints and crowned princes that had been the only ornaments of its bare walls. "In accordance with custom," says M. Augé de Lassus, "the entrance to the Bastille was single and double at the same time; the gate for vehicles, defended by its drawbridge, was flanked by a smaller gate reserved for foot passengers, and this, too, was only accessible when a small drawbridge was lowered."

In the first of the two courtyards of the Bastille, D'Argenson had placed a monumental clock held up by large sculptured figures representing prisoners in chains. The heavy chains fell in graceful curves around the clock-face, as a kind of ornamentation. D'Argenson and his artists had a ferocious taste.

On the morrow of the defeat at St. Quentin,[1] the fear of invasion decided Henri II., under the advice of Coligny, to strengthen the Bastille. It was then, accordingly, that there was constructed, in front of the Saint-Antoine gate, the bastion which was at a later date to be adorned with a garden for the prisoners to walk in.

Around the massive and forbidding prison, in the course of the seventeenth and eighteenth centuries, quite a little town sprang up and flourished, as in the Middle Ages happened around lofty and impressive cathedrals. Barbers, cobblers, drink-sellers, poulterers, cheesemongers, and general dealers had their shops there. These new buildings encroached on the Rue Saint-Antoine, and extended as far as the convent of the Visitation, the chapel of which, converted into a Protestant place of worship, still exists.

"In its latter days," writes M. de Lassus, "the Bastille with its appendages presented an appearance somewhat as follows:—On the Rue Saint-Antoine, a gateway of considerable size, and, with its trophies of arms, making some pretensions to a triumphal arch, gave access to a

[1] The battle fought on August 10, 1557, in which Egmont with a combined force of Spaniards, Flemish, and English (sent by Queen Mary) routed Constable Montmorency and the finest chivalry of France. It was in commemoration of this victory that Philip II. built the palace of the Escurial, shaped like a gridiron because the battle was fought on St. Lawrence's day.—T.

first court skirted with shops, and open, at least during the day, to all comers. People might pass through it freely, but were not allowed to loiter there. Then appeared a second entrance, a double one for horse and foot traffic, each gate defended by its drawbridge. Admittance through this was more difficult, and the sentry's instructions more rigorous; this was the outer guard. As soon as this entrance was passed, one came to the court of the governor, who received the more or less voluntary visitor. On the right stretched the quarters of the governor and his staff, contiguous to the armoury. Then there were the moats, originally supplied by the waters of the Seine—at that time people frequently fell in and were drowned, the moats not being protected by any railing—in later times they were for the most part dry. Then rose the lofty towers of the citadel, encircled, nearly a hundred feet up, by their crown of battlements; and then one found the last drawbridge, most often raised, at any rate before the carriage gate, the door for foot passengers alone remaining accessible, under still more rigorous conditions."

These conditions, so rigorous for contemporaries—the Czar Peter the Great himself found them inflexible—are removed for the historian: thanks to the numerous memoirs left by prisoners, thanks to the documents relating to the administration of the Bastille now in the Arsenal library, and to the correspondence of the lieutenants of police, we shall penetrate into the interior of these well-fenced precincts and follow the life of the prisoners day by day.

In its early days, then, the Bastille was not a prison, though it became such as early as the reign of Charles VI. Yet for two centuries it kept its character as a military citadel. Sometimes the kings gave lodgment there to great personages who were passing through Paris. Louis XI. and Francis I. held brilliant fêtes there, of which the chroniclers speak with admiration.

It is Richelieu who must be considered the founder of the Bastille—the Bastille, that is, as a royal prison, the Bastille of the seventeenth and eighteenth centuries. Before him, imprisonment in the old fortress was merely casual; it is to him that we must trace the conception of the state prison as an instrument of government. Here we shall be arrested by the question, what is to be understood by a state prison? The term, vague and open to discussion, is explained by M. Bournon. "By a state prison—taking the Bastille as a particular instance—must be understood a prison for those who have committed a crime or misdemeanour not provided for by the common law; for those who, rightly or wrongly, have appeared dangerous to the safety of the state, whether the nation itself is concerned, or its head, or a body more or less considerable of citizens, a body sometimes no larger than the family of the suspect. If we add to this class of prisoners personages too conspicuous to be punished for a crime at common law on equal terms with the ordinary malefactor, and for whom it would appear inevitable that an exceptional prison should be reserved, we shall have passed in review the different kinds of delinquents who expiated their misdeeds at the Bastille from the time of Richelieu to the Revolution."

The administration of the Bastille, which, up to the reign of Louis XIII., was entrusted to great lords, dukes, constables, marshals of France—the Marshal de Bassompierre, the Constable de Luynes, the Marshal de Vitry, the Duke of Luxemburg, to mention only the last of them—was placed by Richelieu in the hands of a real jailer, Leclerc du Tremblay, brother of Père Joseph.

Documents throwing any light on the Bastille at the time when the Red Man, as Victor Hugo named

[1] The following unpublished letter from Pontchartrain to Bernaville, intimating his probable nomination as governor of the Bastille, shows exactly what Louis XIV.'s government demanded of the head of the great state prison:—

"Versailles, September 28, 1707.

"I have received your letter of yesterday. I can only repeat what I have already written: to pay constant attention to what goes on in the Bastille; to neglect none of the duties of a good governor; to maintain order and discipline among the soldiers of the garrison, seeing that they keep watch with all the necessary exactitude, and that their wages are regularly paid; to take care that the prisoners are well fed and treated with kindness, preventing them, however, from having any communication with people outside and from writing letters; finally, to be yourself especially prompt in informing me of anything particular that may happen at the Bastille. You will understand that in following such a line of action you cannot but please the king, and perhaps induce him to grant you the post of governor; on my part, you may count on my neglecting no means of representing your services to His Majesty in the proper light.

"I am, &c.,
"PONTCHARTRAIN."

Richelieu, was supreme, are however very rare. An advocate, Maton de la Varenne, published in 1786, in his *Revolutions of Paris*, a letter which ostensibly had been written on December 1, 1642, to Richelieu, at that time ill. In it we read : " I, whom you are causing to rot in the Bastille for having disobeyed your commandment, which would have brought upon my soul condemnation to eternal hell, and would have made me appear in eternity with hands stained with blood——" It is impossible to guarantee the authenticity of this document. To us it appears suspicious, the text having been published at a time when many apocryphal documents were produced as coming from the archives of the Bastille. More worthy of arresting our attention is the " return of the prisoners who are in the château of the Bastille," a document of Richelieu's time which M. Bournon discovered in the archives of the Foreign Office. This catalogue, containing fifty-three names, is the oldest list of prisoners of the Bastille known up to the present time. Among the prisoners several are suspected or convicted of evil designs against " Monsieur le cardinal," some are accused of an intention to " complot," that is, to conspire against the throne, or of being spies. There is an " extravagant " priest, a monk who had " opposed Cluni's election," three hermits, three coiners, the Marquis d'Assigny, condemned to death, but whose punishment had been commuted to perpetual imprisonment, a score or so of lords designated as " madmen, vile scoundrels, evil wretches," or accused of some definite crime, theft or murder; finally, those whose name is followed by the simple note, "Queen-mother," or "Monsieur,"[1] whence we may conclude that the clerk had no exact information about the prisoners of the cardinal. We shall give later the list of the prisoners in the Bastille on the day of its capture, July 14, 1789; and the comparison between the two lists at the two periods, the remotest and the most recent that we could select, will be instructive. We have also, to assist us in forming a judgment of the Bastille in Richelieu's time, the memoirs of Bassompierre and of Laporte, which transport us into a state prison, elegant, we might almost say luxurious, reserved for prisoners of birth and breeding, where they lived observing all social usages in their mutual relations, paying and returning calls. But the Bastille preserved its military character for many more years, and among the prisoners we find especially a number of officers punished for breaches of discipline. Prisoners of war were confined there, and foreign personages of high rank arrested by way of reprisal, secret agents and spies employed in France by hostile nations; finally, powerful lords who had incurred the king's displeasure. The court intrigues under Richelieu and Mazarin contributed to the diversion of the Bastille from its original intention: they began to incarcerate there *valets de chambre* who had somehow become mixed up in the plots of sovereigns.

Religious persecution was revived by the government

[1] The appellation of the eldest brother of the reigning king.—T.

of Louis XIV., and ere long a whole world of gazetteers and "novelists," the journalists of the period, were seen swarming like flies in the sun. Louis XIV. was not precisely a stickler for the liberty of the press, but on the other hand he shrank from cooping up men of letters, Jansenists and Protestants convinced of the truth of their beliefs, pell-mell with the vagabonds and thiefs confined at Bicêtre, Saint-Lazare, and the other prisons of Paris. He threw open to them, too generously no doubt, the portals of his château in the Suburb Saint-Antoine, where they mixed with young men of family undergoing a mild course of the Bastille at the request of their parents, and with quarrelsome nobles whom the marshals of France, anxious to avoid duels, used to send there to forget their animosities. Further, the reign of Louis XIV. was marked by some great trials which produced a strange and appalling impression, and threw around the accused a halo of mystery—trials for magic and sorcery, cases of poisoning and base coining. The accused parties in these cases were confined in the Bastille. And here we encounter a fresh departure from the primitive character of the old fortress; prisoners were sent there whose cases were tried by the regularly constituted judges. Henceforth prisoners who appeared before the court of the Arsenal were divided between the Bastille and the fortress of Vincennes.

This is the grand epoch in the history of the Bastille: it is now a veritable prison of state. Writers can speak of its "nobleness." It shows itself to us in colours at once charming and awe-inspiring, brilliant, majestic, now filled with sounds of merriment, now veiled with an appalling silence. From the gloomy regions within the massive walls there come to us the sounds of song and laughter mingled with cries of despair, with sobs and tears. This is the period of the Iron Mask: the period when the governor receives mysterious letters from the court. "I beg you, sir, to see that, if anyone comes to ask for news of the prisoner whom Desgrez conducted to the Bastille this morning by order of the king, nothing be said about him, and that, if possible, in accordance with the intention of His Majesty and the accompanying instructions, no one may get to know him or even his name." "M. de Bernaville (the name of one of the governors of the Bastille), having given orders for the conveyance of an important prisoner to the prison of my château of the Bastille, I send this letter to inform you of my intention that you receive him there and keep him closely guarded until further orders, warning you not to permit him, under any pretext whatever, to hold communication with any person, either by word of mouth or in writing." The prisoners surrounded with so absolute a silence almost all belonged to the same category, namely, distinguished spies, who seem to have been rather numerous in France at the full tide of Louis XIV.'s wars, and who were hunted down with an eagerness which grew in proportion as fortune frowned on the royal armies. We read in the Journal kept by the King's lieutenant, Du Junca: "On Wednesday, December 22, about ten o'clock in the morning, M. de la Coste, provost of the King's armies, came here, bringing and leaving in our custody a prisoner whom for greater secrecy he caused to enter by our new gate, which allows us to pass into or out of the garden of the Arsenal at all hours—the which prisoner, M. d'Estingen by name, a German, but married in England, was received by the governor by order of the King sent by the hand of the Marquis de Barbezieux, with explicit instructions to keep the prisoner's presence a secret and to prevent him from holding communication with anyone, in speech or writing : the which prisoner is a widower, without children, a man of intelligence, and doing a brisk trade in news of what is happening in France, sending his information to Germany, England, and Holland : a gentlemanly spy." On February 10, 1710, Pontchartrain wrote to Bernaville, governor of the Bastille : "I cannot refrain from telling you that you and the Chevalier de la Croix speak a good deal too much and too openly about the foreign prisoners you have. Secrecy and mystery is one of your first duties, as I must ask you to remember. Neither D'Argenson nor any other than those I have apprized you of should see these prisoners. Give explicit warning to the Abbé Renaudot and to de la Croix of the necessity of maintaining an inviolable and impenetrable secrecy."

It happened also at that period that a prisoner remained in complete ignorance of the reason of his incarceration: "The prisoner at the Bastille named J. J. du Vacquay," writes Louvois to the governor, "has complained to the King that he has been kept there for thirteen years without knowing the reason: be good enough to let me know what minister signed the warrant under which he is detained, so that I may report to His Majesty."

As the greater part of the papers relating to the arrest were destroyed as soon as the incarceration was effected, it sometimes happened that in certain cases the reasons were not known even in the offices of the ministers. Thus Seignelay writes to the governor, M. de Besmaus: "The King has commanded me to write and ask you who is a certain prisoner named Dumesnil, how long he has been at the Bastille, and for what reason he was placed there." "The demoiselle de Mirail, a prisoner at the Bastille, having demanded her liberty of the King, His Majesty has instructed me to write and ask you the reason of her detention; if you know it, be good enough to inform me at your earliest convenience." Again, we find Louvois writing to the same effect: "I am sending you a letter from M. Coquet, in regard to which the King has commanded me to ask who signed the warrant under which he was sent to the Bastille, and whether you know the reason of his being sent there." "Sir, I am writing a line merely to ask you to let me know who is Piat de la Fontaine, who has been five years at the Bastille, and whether you do not remember why he was placed there."

Letters of this kind are, it is true, very rare; yet if one compares the state of things they disclose with the extraordinary comfort and luxury with which the prisoners were surrounded, they help to characterize the celebrated prison at this epoch of its history, namely, the seventeenth century.

In 1667 the office of lieutenant of police had been created. The first to hold the title was Gabriel Nicolas de la Reynie, a man of the greatest worth. It is very important to note that under the *ancien régime* the lieutenant of police had a double function, being at the same time a subordinate of the minister of Paris [1] and a member of the Châtelet.[2] His duties were thus of a twofold nature, administrative and judicial. Now the Bastille, as a state prison, was more especially an administrative institution; but gradually, owing to the character of the persons brought there as prisoners, it became difficult to avoid turning it also into a judicial institution, and the minister of Paris became accustomed to delegate his subordinate, the lieutenant of police, to conduct the examination of the prisoners at the Bastille. Though La Reynie took practically the whole respon-

---

[1] Under the *ancien régime*, there being no Minister of the Interior (Home Secretary), each of the ministers (the War Minister, Minister for Foreign Affairs, &c.) had a part of France under his charge. The Minister of Paris was usually what we should call the Lord Chamberlain.—T.

[2] The court which up to the time of the Revolution was the seat of justice, presided over by the Provost of Paris. It held its sittings in the castle known as the Châtelet.—T.

sibility of the administration of the Bastille, his visits to the prison itself were nevertheless relatively rare, and on every occasion a permit signed by Louis XIV. or by Colbert was necessary.

La Reynie was succeeded by D'Argenson. Under him the powers of the lieutenant of police were very largely extended, and the Bastille was comprised within his jurisdiction. Henceforth the lieutenant of police will enter the state prison whenever it seems good to him, as lord and master, accompanied by his subordinates at the Châtelet, clerks and inspectors of police; the prisoners will be in direct and constant communication with him, and he will make an inspection of all the chambers at least once a year. We find that at every change in the lieutenancy of police, it sufficed for the minister of Paris to send the name of the new officer to the governor. Dating from this period, the prison in the Suburb Saint-Antoine remained under the authority of a magistrate.

The Regency was a transition period between the reigns of Louis XIV. and Louis XV., and there was a corresponding transition period in the history of the Bastille. The incarcerations were less numerous and less rigorous, but the rule of the prison lost something of that aristocratic air which had characterized it. The most important episode in the history of the Bastille during the Regency was the incarceration of those who were accused of complicity in the Cellamare conspiracy. Among these was Mdlle de Launay, later to be known as Madame de Staal. She has left some charming pages about her imprisonment, in which we find, related with a fluent and subtle pen, the little romance which we proceed to outline.

Mdlle de Launay was secretary to the Duchess of Maine. She had had some part in drawing up the scheme of the Cellamare conspiracy, which, if it had succeeded, would have placed the king of Spain on the throne of France. On December 10, 1718, the Regent sent her, with several of her accomplices, to the Bastille, less with the idea of punishing her for machinations against the state than to obtain from her details of the conspiracy. At that period of her life she was of but moderate fortune and rank, and it would not have been strange if she had been treated with rigour. She found at the Bastille, on the contrary, unexpected comfort and consideration. In her *Memoirs*, she writes that her sojourn at the Bastille was the pleasantest time of her life. Her maid, Rondel, was permitted to live with her. She was installed in a veritable suite of rooms. She complained of the mice there, and a cat was given her, to drive out the mice and provide some amusement. By and by there were kittens, and the sportive tricks of the numerous little family cheered her wonderfully, she said. Mdlle de Launay was regularly invited to dine with the governor; she spent her days in writing and card-playing. The king's lieutenant, Maisonrouge, a man well on in years, who held, after the governor, the first place in the administration of the château, conceived a profound and pathetic passion for the fair prisoner. He declared that nothing would give him greater happiness than to make her his wife. His apartments happened to be near those of Mdlle de Launay. Unhappily for the king's lieutenant, there was in the neighbourhood a third suite, occupied by a young and brilliant nobleman, the Chevalier de Ménil, who also was implicated in the Cellamare affair. The fair prisoner was not acquainted with him. Maisonrouge impresses us as a man of great dignity, and rare nobility of character. He spoke to the two young prisoners about each other, hoping, by bringing them into communication, to provide them with fresh distractions, more particularly the lady, whom he loved. The Chevalier de Ménil and Mdlle de Launay could not see each other; they had never met. They began by exchanging epistles in verse. Like everything that came from her pen, the verses of Mdlle de Launay were full of animation and charm. The good Maisonrouge played post between them, happy to see his little friend's delight in the diversion she owed to him. It was not long before the verses carried from one room to the other by Maisonrouge began to speak of love, and this love—surprising as it may seem, but not difficult to understand in the sequestered life of the Bastille—ere long became real in the consciousness of the young people, who saw each other in imagination under the most charming colours. Maisonrouge was soon induced to contrive an interview between them. It is a delightful moment. The two captives had never seen each other, yet loved each other passionately : what will their mutual impressions be ? Mdlle de Launay's impression, when she saw the gay chevalier, was of unmixed enthusiasm ; the chevalier's, maybe, was more subdued ; but if it is true, as someone has said, that to nuns the gardener represents mankind, to a prisoner every young woman must be an exquisite creature. The interviews continued under the benevolent eye of Maisonrouge, who watched the development of Mdlle de Launay's love for Ménil—the love of the girl whom he himself loved intensely, but whose happiness he preferred to his own. There are delightful details which may be found delightfully described in Mdlle de Launay's *Memoirs*. It is M. Bournon's opinion that, according to the testimony of Mdlle de Launay herself, this idyll of the Bastille had " the dénouement that might have been foretold." We have caught no hint of the sort in the *Memoirs* of Madame de Staal, but then, M. Bournon is no doubt the better psychologist. At any rate, the governor of the Bastille got wind of the diversions of the lovers. He put his foot down. Ménil was transferred to a distant tower, Mdlle de Launay shed tears, and, incredible as it seems, Maisonrouge, while redoubling his efforts to please her, sympathized with her lot to the point of arranging fresh and more difficult interviews with the sparkish chevalier. Mdlle de Launay left the prison in the spring of 1720, after having sent to the Regent a detailed statement of the facts of the conspiracy, which hitherto she had refused to furnish. Once at liberty, she vainly implored the Chevalier de Ménil to fulfil his pledges and make her his wife. Maisonrouge died in the following year, of disappointment, says the gay coquette, at his failure to get from her, during her imprisonment, the promise of marriage which now she would have been glad enough to fulfil.

It seems as though under the Regency everything at the Bastille turned on love—a reflection of the epoch itself. The young Duke de Richelieu was locked up there because he did not love his wife. The brilliant nobleman was kept under lock and key for several weeks, "in solitude and gloom," he says, when suddenly the door of his room flew open and Madame de Richelieu appeared, a wonder of grace, brightness and charm: "The fair angel," writes the duke, "who flew from heaven to earth to set Peter free was not so radiant."

We have seen how the Bastille had been transformed from a military citadel into a prison of state. We shall now witness, under the government of the Duke of Orleans, another transformation, betokened by an event which is of little apparent importance. The Duke de Richelieu was imprisoned in the Bastille a second time as the result of a duel: a judge of the Parlement went there to question him and the Parlement tried his case. The Parlement[1] at the Bastille, in the prison of the king! From that moment the fortress continued year by year to grow more like our modern

[1] A judicial, not a legislative body. It was constantly in antagonism to the king.—T.

prisons. "Under the Cardinal de Fleury," writes La Harpe, "this famous château was inhabited by hardly any but Jansenist writers: it then became the enforced residence of champions of philosophy and authors of clandestine satires, and acted as a foil to their obscurity and shame." It became increasingly the practice to confine there accused persons whose cases were regularly tried at the Châtelet or even before the Parlement. By the second half of the eighteenth century accused persons had come to be incarcerated in the Bastille by direct order of the Châtelet, which would have seemed incredible to a contemporary of Louis XIV. The summoning officer would post himself before the towers, and there, while the prisoner pressed his head close against the bars of the window, the officer would shout the terms of the writ at him across the moat. The advocates defending the accused obtained permission to go and consult their clients, and they were the only persons who were permitted to interview the prisoners in private. On the appointed day the prisoner was transferred to the law courts quietly and by night to avoid the curiosity of the crowd.

Under Louis XVI. the judges of the Parlement visited the Bastille as they visited the other prisons; at length the minister Breteuil sent instructions to the officials informing them that no more *lettres de cachet* would be issued without stating the duration of the penalty to which the guilty person was condemned and the grounds for his punishment. The Bastille was now merely a prison like the others, except that the prisoners were better treated there.

In 1713 Voysin, the Secretary of State, wrote to D'Argenson : "Beaumanielle is not sufficiently deserving of consideration to warrant his removal from the Châtelet to the Bastille." La Harpe has well described the transformation which from this time came over the great state prison by saying that, from the beginning of the century, none of the prisoners who had been placed there " had merited the honour." His remark receives corroboration from Linguet : " It is not, in these latter days especially, for criminals of state that the Bastille is reserved : it has become in some sort the antichambre of the conciergerie."

If the glories of the Bastille paled as it grew older, on the other hand torture, which, it is true, had never been applied except by order of the courts, had completely disappeared. From the beginning of the eighteenth century, the cells and chains were merely a temporary punishment reserved for insubordinate prisoners : from the accession of Louis XVI. they had fallen into disuse. Breteuil forbade any person whatever to be placed in the cells, which were the rooms on the lowest floor of each tower, a sort of damp and gloomy vaults. On September 11, 1775, Malesherbes writes : " No prisoner should be refused material for reading and writing. The abuse it is pretended that they may make of it cannot be dangerous, confined so closely as they are. Nor should any refusal be made to the desire of such as may wish to devote themselves to other occupations, provided they do not require you to leave in their hands tools of which they might avail themselves to effect their escape. If any of them should wish to write to his family and his friends, he must be permitted to receive replies, and to send replies to their letters after having read them. In all this you must be guided by your prudence and your humanity." The reading of the gazettes, formerly rigidly forbidden, was now authorised.

It must further be remarked that the number of prisoners confined in the Bastille was not so large as might be thought. During the whole reign of Louis XVI. the Bastille received no more than two hundred and forty prisoners, an average of sixteen a year; while it had room for forty-two in separate apartments.

Under Louis XIV., at the period when the government was most liberal in dispensing its *lettres de cachet*, an average of only thirty prisoners a year entered the château, and their captivity was for the most part of short duration. Dumouriez informs us in his *Memoirs* that during his detention he had never more than eighteen fellow prisoners, and that more than once he had only six. M. Alfred Bégis has drawn up a list of the prisoners detained in the Bastille from 1781 to 1789. In May, 1788, it contained twenty-seven prisoners, the highest figure reached during these eight years; in September, 1782, it contained ten; in April, 1783, seven; in June of the same year, seven; in December, 1788, nine; in February, 1789, nine; at the time of its capture, July 14, 1789, there were seven.

True, not only men were locked up in the Bastille, but also books when they appeared dangerous. The royal warrant under which they were incarcerated was even drawn up on the model of the *lettres de cachet*. M. Bournon has published a specimen of these. The books were shut up in a closet between the towers of the Treasury and the County, over an old passage communicating with the bastion. In 1733 the lieutenant of police instructed the governor of the Bastille to receive at the château "all the apparatus of a clandestine printing-press which had been seized in a chamber of the Saint-Victor abbey: the which you will be good enough to have placed in the store room of the Bastille." When the books ceased to appear dangerous, they were set at liberty. In this way the *Encyclopædia*[1] was liberated after a detention of some years.

We have just seen that during the reign of Louis XVI. the Bastille did not receive more than sixteen prisoners a year, on an average. Several of these were only detained for a few days. From 1783 to 1789 the Bastille remained almost empty, and would have been absolutely empty if it had not been decided to place there prisoners who should properly have been

[1] The famous Encyclopædia edited by D'Alembert and Diderot. It occupied twenty years of the life of the latter, and went through many vicissitudes; its free criticism of existing institutions provoking the enmity of the government. Voltaire was one of its largest contributors.—T.

elsewhere. As early as February, 1784, the fortress of Vincennes, which served as a sort of overflow pipe to the Bastille, had been shut for lack of prisoners. The system of *lettres de cachet* was slipping away into the past. On the other hand, the Bastille was a source of great expense to the King. The governor alone received 60,000 livres annually. When you add the salaries and board of the officers of the garrison, the turnkeys, the physicians, the surgeon, the apothecary, the chaplains; when you add the food—this alone in 1774 came to 67,000 livres—and the clothing of the prisoners, and the upkeep of the buildings, the total will appear outrageous, for the figures given above must be tripled to represent the value of the present day. So Necker, seeing that the Bastille was of no further utility, thought of suppressing it "for economy's sake,"[1] and he was not the only one in high places to speak of this suppression. The Carnavalet[2] museum possesses a scheme drawn up in 1784 by Corbet, the superintending architect to the city of Paris, whence the project has an official character: it is a scheme for a "Place Louis XVI." to be opened up on the site of the old fortress. We learn from Millin

---

[1] This raised Linguet's indignation. "The consideration of this enormous expense has given to some ministers, among others to M. Necker, a notion of reform; if this should come to anything, it would be very disgraceful to spring from no other cause. 'Suppress the Bastille out of economy!' said on this subject, a few days ago, one of the youngest and most eloquent orators of England."

[2] The Hôtel Carnavalet, museum in Paris, where a large number of documents and books are preserved relating to the history of the city. —T.

that other artists "were occupied with a scheme for erecting a monument on the site of the Bastille." One of these schemes deserves special mention. Seven of the eight towers were to be destroyed, the eighth to remain standing, but in a significant state of dilapidation: on the site of the demolished towers a monument was to be erected to the glory of Louis XVI. This monument was to consist of a pedestal formed by piling up chains and bolts taken from the state prison, above which would rise a statue of the king, one hand extended towards the ruined tower with the gesture of a deliverer. It is to be regretted, if not for the beauty, at least for the picturesqueness of Paris, that this scheme was never put into execution. Davy de Chavigné, king's counsellor and auditor to the treasury, was allowed to present to the Royal Academy of Architecture, at its sitting on June 8, 1789, "a plan for a monument on the site of the Bastille, to be decreed by the States General to Louis XVI. as the restorer of the public liberty." On this subject the famous sculptor Houdon wrote to Chavigné: "I am very anxious for the plan to be adopted. The idea of erecting a monument to liberty on the very spot where slavery has reigned up to the present, appears to me particularly well conceived, and well calculated to inspire genius. I shall think myself only too fortunate to be among the artists who will celebrate the epoch of the regeneration of France."

We have seen prints, long anterior to 1789—one of them the frontispiece of the edition of Linguet's *Memoirs* that appeared in 1783—representing Louis XVI. extending his hand towards the lofty towers, which workmen are in the act of demolishing.

Among the archives of the Bastille are preserved two reports drawn up in 1788 by the king's lieutenant, Puget, the most important personage in the fortress after the governor. He proposes the suppression of the state prison, the demolition of the old château, and the sale of the ground for the benefit of the crown. It may be said of these schemes, as of the plan of the architect Corbet, that they would not have been propounded if they had not been approved in high places.

Further, in the year 1784, an ardent supporter of the old state of things cried: " Oh! if our young monarch ever committed a fault so great, if he so far belied the most ancient usages of this government, if it were possible that one day he could be tempted to destroy you " (the author is apostrophizing the Bastille) " to raise on your ruins a monument to the liberator-king. . . ." The demolition of the Bastille was decided on; and it would have been accomplished as a government undertaking but for the outbreak of the Revolution.

From January 1 to July 14, 1789, that is to say for more than six months, only one solitary prisoner entered the Bastille; and what a prisoner!—Réveillon, the paper manufacturer of the Suburb Saint-Antoine, who was shut up on May 1 at his own request, in order to escape the fury of the mob. The same year, the lieutenant of police, de Crosne, made an inspection of the Bastille, accompanied by a judge of the Parlement; their object was to arrange officially about the destruction of the state prison.

Thus, on the eve of the Revolution, the Bastille no longer existed, though its towers were still standing.

The victors of the 14th of July set free seven prisoners: four forgers whose arrest had been ordered by the Châtelet, whose case had been regularly tried, and whose proper place was an ordinary prison; two madmen who ought to have been at Charenton; and the Comte de Solages, a young nobleman who had been guilty of a monstrous crime over which it was desired to throw a veil out of regard for his family; he was maintained on a pension paid by his father. The conquerors of the Bastille destroyed an old fortified castle: the state prison no longer existed. They "broke in an open door." That was said of them even in 1789.

CHAPTER III.

LIFE IN THE BASTILLE.

HAVING sketched rapidly and with bold strokes the outlines of the history of the Bastille from its foundation to its fall, we intend to show how the rule to which prisoners in the fortress of the Suburb Saint-Antoine were submitted underwent its own process of transformation, parallel with the transformation of the prison itself. To understand the facts which follow, and which are of a kind to astound the mind of everyone in these days, it is necessary to remember what we have already said as to the character of the Bastille. It was the prison of luxury, the aristocratic prison of the *ancien régime*, the *prison de luxe* at a period when it was no dishonour, as we shall see later, to be confined there. We must remember the phrase of the minister of Paris writing to D'Argenson, in regard to a personage of but modest rank, that this individual did not deserve "consideration" enough to be put in the Bastille. Let us reflect on this observation of Mercier in his excellent *Pictures of Paris*: "The people fear the Châtelet more than the Bastille. Of the latter they have no dread, because it is almost unknown to them."

We have shown how the Bastille, originally a military citadel, had become a prison of state; then, little by little, had approximated to the ordinary prisons, until the day when it died a natural death ere it could be assassinated. The same transformation took place in the treatment of the prisoners. Midway in the seventeenth century, the Bastille had none of the characteristics of a prison, but was simply a château in which the king caused certain of his subjects to sojourn, for one cause or another. They lived there just as they thought proper, furnishing their rooms according to their fancy with their own furniture, indulging their tastes in regard to food at their own expense, and waited on by their own servants. When a prisoner was rich he could live at the Bastille in princely style; when he was poor, he lived there very wretchedly. When the prisoner had no property at all, the king did not for that reason give him furniture or food; but he gave him money which he might use as seemed good to him in providing himself with furniture and food : money of which he could retain a part—a number of prisoners did not fail to do so—these savings becoming his own property. This system, the character of which it is important to recognize, underwent gradual modification during the course of the seventeenth and eighteenth centuries, approximating, without ever becoming identical with, the system of our modern prisons. Thus the king, instead of granting pensions individually to the poorest of the prisoners, came to endow the Bastille with a certain fixed number of pensions for the less fortunate prisoners. The recipients of these pensions continued to enjoy them for long years, and if they did not wish the whole of the money to be expended on their support, the balance was handed over to them. So we see certain individuals getting little fortunes together by the mere fact of their having been prisoners in the Bastille—a circumstance which has so much surprised historians because they have not sought its cause. It even happened that prisoners, when their liberation was announced to them, asked to remain a little longer in order to swell their savings, a favour which was sometimes granted them. In the course of the eighteenth century the money destined to the maintenance of the prisoners at the Bastille could not be diverted from its purpose; the prisoners were no longer able to appropriate a part; the whole sum had to be expended.

It was only in the second half of the seventeenth century that the king had some rooms at the Bastille furnished for such prisoners as were without means of procuring furniture themselves. And it is very interesting to note that it was only at the extreme end of the century, under the administration of Saint-Mars, that certain apartments of the Bastille were arranged in the prison style with bars and bolts. Until then they had been simply the rooms of a stronghold.[1]

---

[1] It may be noted that the different escapes contributed to the gradual tightening of the rules of the Bastille. After the escape of the Comte de Bucquoy, such ornaments as the prisoners could attach

Let us follow the prisoner from his entrance to his exit.

When the *lettre de cachet* had been signed, it was usually a sort of sheriff's officer who effected the arrest. He appeared in company with five or six men-at-arms, and signified the arrest by touching his quarry with a white staff. A coach was in waiting. The police officer politely begged the person he was instructed to secure to step into the coach, and took his place beside him. And, according to the testimony of various memoirs, while the vehicle was rolling along with lowered blinds, there was a pleasant conversational exchange of courtesies up to the moment of the prisoner's finding himself within the walls of the Bastille. A certain Lafort was living in furnished apartments with a young and pretty Englishwoman whom he had abducted, when one evening, about sunset, a police officer arrived. The coach was at the door. Preliminaries were settled on both sides with as much politeness as if a visit or an evening party had been the topic of discussion. They all got into the vehicle, even the young man's lackey who, beguiled by appearances, mounted behind. Arrived at the Bastille, the lackey lost no time in descending to open the door: there was general astonishment, especially on the part of the poor servant, when he learnt that since he had entered the Bastille along with his master, he must stay with him.

cords to were at once removed, and knives were taken from them; after the escape of Allègre and Latude, bars of iron were placed in the chimneys, and so forth.

LIFE IN THE BASTILLE

Most often the officer and his companions surprised their quarry early in the morning, on rising from bed. Imagine then the coach with the prisoner and the police officer inside, arriving before the Bastille, in the first court in front of the castle keep. "Who goes there?" cries the sentinel. "The king's writ!" replies the officer. At this, the shops we have seen attached to the flanks of the château are bound at once to be shut. The soldiers on guard have to turn their faces to the wall, or perhaps to pull their hats over their eyes. The coach passes the outpost, a bell sounds. "Advance!' cries the officer on duty. The drawbridge is lowered and the coach rattles over the stout iron-clamped boards. For greater secrecy, spies and prisoners of war were taken in by a private door leading to the gardens of the Arsenal.

Officers and noblemen presented themselves before the Bastille alone, unless they were accompanied by relatives or friends. "It is my intention," the king had written to them, "that you betake yourselves to my château of the Bastille." And no one dreamt of declining the royal invitation. Further, when the governor desired to transfer one of them from one prison to another, he contented himself with telling him so. We find in the Journal of Du Junca, king's lieutenant [1] at the

---

[1] The second of the four principal officers of the Bastille. The officers were: (1) the governor; (2) the king's lieutenant; (3) the major; (4) the adjutant. There was also a doctor, a surgeon, a confessor, &c. The garrison consisted of Invalides.—T.

Bastille, several notes like the following: "Monday, December 26, 1695, about ten o'clock in the morning, M. de Villars, lieutenant-colonel of the regiment of Vosges infantry, came and reported himself a prisoner, as ordered by M. Barbezieux, though he was a prisoner in the citadel of Grenoble, whence he came direct without being brought by anyone."[1] On the arrival of the prisoner, the king's lieutenant, accompanied by the captain of the gates, came to receive him as he got out of his carriage. The officers of the château at once led the new-comer into the presence of the governor, who received him civilly, invited him to sit down, and after having endorsed the *lettre de cachet* conversed with him for some time. Under Louis XIV. the governor in most cases even kept his new guest, as well as the persons who had accompanied him, to lunch or dinner. Meanwhile his quarters had been got ready. We read in Du Junca's Journal that on January 26, 1695, a certain De Courlandon, a colonel of cavalry, presented himself for incarceration at the Bastille. There being no room ready to receive him, the governor asked him to go and pass the night in a neighbouring inn, at the sign of the

---

[1] The most surprising instance is that of an Englishman, who returned spontaneously from England to become a prisoner in the Bastille. "On Thursday, May 22, 1693, at nightfall, M. de Jones, an Englishman, returned from England, having come back to prison for reasons concerning the king's service. He was located outside the château, in a little room where M. de Besmaus keeps his library, above his office, and he is not to appear for some days for his examination, and is to be taken great care of."—Du Junca's Journal.

Crown, and to return next day. "Whereupon M. de Courlandon did not fail to return about eleven o'clock in the morning, having dined with M. de Besmaus (the governor), and in the afternoon he entered the château."

The reader will not be surprised at learning that the prospect of incarceration at the Bastille did not always strike the future prisoner with terror. We read in the *Memoirs* of the Duke de Lauzun :[1] "Scolded for two hours on end by everybody who fancied himself entitled to do so, I thought I could not do better than go to Paris and await developments. A few hours after my arrival, I received a letter from my father telling me that it had been decided to put us all in the Bastille, and that I should probably be arrested during the night. I determined at least to finish gaily, so I invited some pretty girls from the Opera to supper, so that I might await the officer without impatience. Seeing that he did not arrive, I determined on the bold move of going to Fontainebleau and joining the king's hunt. He did not speak to me once during the chase, which was such a confirmation of our disgrace that on our return no one gave us the customary salute. But I did not lose heart; in the evening I was in attendance, and the king came to me. 'You are all,' he said, 'hotheaded rips, but funny dogs all the same; come along and have supper, and bring M. de Guéméné and the Chevalier de Luxembourg.'"

---

[1] This was not the Lauzun already mentioned, but his nephew, Armand Louis de Gontaut, duke de Biron (1747-1793), who was notorious throughout Europe for his gallantries.—T.

Before the new arrival was installed in the chamber prepared for him, he was taken to the great council hall, where he was requested to empty his pockets. Only notorious rogues were searched. If the prisoner had upon him money, jewels, or other articles such as knives and scissors, the use of which was not allowed by the regulations, they were done up in a parcel which he himself sealed, with his own seal if he had one ; if not, with the seal of the Bastille. Finally, he was conducted to the room reserved for him.

Each of the eight towers of the Bastille contained four or five stories of rooms or cells. The worst of these rooms were on the lowest floor, and these were what were called the " cells,"—octagonal vaults, cold and damp, partly under ground ; the walls, grey with mould, were bare from floor to ceiling, the latter a groined arch. A bench and a bed of straw covered with a paltry coverlet, formed the whole appointments. Daylight feebly flickered through the vent-hole opening on to the moat. When the Seine was in flood, the water came through the walls and swamped the cells ; and then any prisoners who might happen to be in them were removed. During the reign of Louis XIV. the cells were sometimes occupied by prisoners of the lowest class and criminals condemned to death. Later, under Louis XV., the cells ceased to be used except as a place of punishment for insubordinate prisoners who assaulted their guardians or fellow-prisoners, or for turnkeys and sentinels of the château who had committed breaches of discipline. They stayed in the cells for a short time in irons. The cells had fallen into disuse by the time the Revolution broke out; since the first ministry of Necker, it had been forbidden to confine in them any one whatever, and none of the warders questioned on July 18 remembered having seen any one placed in them. The two prisoners, Tavernier and Béchade, whom the conquerors of the 14th of July found in one of these dungeons, had been placed there, at the moment of the attack, by the officers of the château, for fear lest amid the rain of bullets some harm should befall them.

The worst rooms after the cells were the *calottes*, the rooms on the floor above. In summer the heat was extreme in them, and in winter the cold, in spite of the stoves. They were octagons whose ceilings, as the name implies, were shaped like a skull-cap. High enough in the centre, they gradually diminished in height towards the sides. It was impossible to stand upright except in the middle of the room.

The prisoners were only placed in the cells and *calottes* under exceptional circumstances. Every tower had two or three floors of lofty and airy chambers, and in these the prisoners lived. They were octagons from fifteen to sixteen feet in diameter and from fifteen to twenty feet high. Light entered through large windows approached by three steps. We have said that it was only towards the end of Louis XIV.'s reign that these rooms were arranged like prison cells with bars and bolts. They were warmed with open fireplaces or stoves. The ceiling was whitewashed, the floor of brick. On the walls the prisoners had chalked verses, mottoes, and designs.

One artistic prisoner amused himself by decorating the bare walls with paintings. The governor, delighted at seeing him thus find relaxation, moved him from room to room; when he had finished filling one with his designs and arabesques, he was placed in another. Some of these rooms were decorated with portraits of Louis XIV. placed above the chimney-piece, a characteristic detail which helps to show what the Bastille was at this period: the château of the king, where the king received a certain number of his subjects as his willing or unwilling guests.

The best rooms in the Bastille were those that were fitted up in the eighteenth century for the accommodation of the staff. These were what were called the "suites." In these were placed invalids and prisoners of distinction.

At the beginning of the eighteenth century, the furniture of these apartments was still extremely simple: they were absolutely empty. The reason of this we have indicated above. "I arrived," says Madame de Staal, "at a room where there was nothing but four walls, very filthy, and daubed all over by my predecessors for want of something better to do. It was so destitute of furniture that someone went and got a little straw chair for me to sit on, and two stones to support a lighted faggot, and a little candle-end was neatly stuck on the wall to give me light."

The prisoners sent to their own homes for a table, bed,

and chair, or they hired these from the upholsterer of the Bastille. When they had nothing to bless themselves with, the government, as we have already said, did not provide them with furniture. It gave them money, sometimes considerable sums, which permitted them to adorn their rooms after their own fancy. This was the case in regard to all prisoners up to 1684. At this date the king ordered the administration to supply furniture to those of the prisoners whose detention was to be kept secret, for, by getting in bedding from their own houses or the houses of friends, they made known their arrest. D'Argenson had half a dozen of the rooms permanently furnished, others were furnished under Louis XV.; under Louis XVI., almost all were furnished. The appointments were very modest: a bed of green baize with curtains, one or two tables, several chairs, fire-dogs, a shovel, and a small pair of tongs. But after having undergone examination, the prisoner retained the right of getting in furniture from outside. And in this way the rooms of the prisoners were sometimes adorned with great elegance. Madame de Staal relates that she had hers hung with tapestry; the Marquis de Sade covered the bare walls with long and brilliant hangings: other prisoners ornamented their rooms with family portraits: they procured chests of drawers, desks, round tables, dressing-cases, armchairs, cushions in Utrecht velvet; the inventories of articles belonging to the prisoners show that they managed to secure everything they thought necessary. The Abbé Brigault, who was imprisoned at the same time as Madame de Staal and for the same affair, brought into the Bastille five armchairs, two pieces of tapestry, eleven serge hangings, eight chairs, a bureau, a small table, three pictures, &c. The list of effects taken out of the Bastille by the Comte de Belle-Isle when he was set at liberty includes a library consisting of 333 volumes and ten atlases, a complete service of fine linen and plate for the table, a bed furnished with gold-bordered red damask, four pieces of tapestry on antique subjects, two mirrors, a screen of gold-bordered red damask matching the bed, two folding screens, two armchairs with cushions, an armchair in leather, three chairs in tapestry, an overmantel of gilt copper, tables, drawers, stands, candlestick of plated copper, &c. We might multiply examples, even from among prisoners of middle station.

It was the rule that prisoners newly arrived at the Bastille should be examined within twenty-four hours. It sometimes happened, however, that one or another remained for two or three weeks before appearing before the magistrate. The Châtelet commissioner, specially delegated to the Bastille for these examinations, founded his questions on notes supplied him by the lieutenant of police, who, indeed, often went in person to see the prisoners. A special commission was appointed for affairs of importance. Dumouriez says that he was examined after nine hours of detention by three commissioners: "The president was an old councillor of state named Marville, a man of intelligence, but coarse and sarcastic. The second was M. de Sartine, lieutenant of police and councillor of state, a man of polish and refinement. The third was a *maître des requêtes*[1] named Villevaux, a very insincere and disputatious fellow. The clerk, who had more intelligence than any of them, was an advocate named Beaumont."

We have found many instances of prisoners who spoke in high terms of their judges. And it cannot be said that prisoners at the Bastille escaped judgment. A Châtelet commissioner examined them and sent the official report of his examination, with a statement of his opinion, to the lieutenant of police. He decided whether the arrest should be sustained. Moreover, it would be a mistake to compare the lieutenant of police under the *ancien régime* with the prefect of police of to-day; the lieutenants of police, selected from former *maîtres des requêtes*, had a judicial character: the documents of the period call them "magistrates"; they issued decrees without appeal and pronounced penal sentences, even condemning to the galleys; they were at the same time justices of the peace with an extensive jurisdiction. In addition to the examination held on the entrance of a prisoner, the lieutenants of police, in the course of their frequent visits, addressed to the

[1] An official of the royal council, whose function originally was to examine and report on petitions to the king. He became a sort of superior magistrate's clerk.—T.

ministers of Paris reports on the prisoners,—reports in which they discussed the evidence, and which constituted veritable judgments.

When the prisoner was recognized as innocent, a new *lettre de cachet* soon set him at liberty. The verdict of "no true bill" often supervened with a rapidity which the decisions of our police magistrates would do well to emulate. A certain Barbier, who entered the Bastille on February 15, 1753, was found not guilty and set at liberty the next day. Of the 279 persons imprisoned in the Bastille during the last fifteen years of the *ancien régime*, thirty-eight benefited by the dropping of the indictment.

Finally—and here is a point on which the new method might well model itself on that of the Bastille—when a detention was recognized as unjust, the victim was indemnified. A great number of examples might be mentioned. An advocate named Subé left the Bastille on June 18, 1767, after a detention of eighteen days; he had been falsely accused of the authorship of a book against the king, and received compensation to the tune of 3000 livres, more than £240 of our money. A certain Pereyra, imprisoned in the Bastille from November 7, 1771, to April 12, 1772, and then from July 1 to September 26, 1774, having been found to be innocent, was reinstated in all his property, and received from the king a life pension of 1200 livres, more than £100 to-day. A certain number of those accused in the Canada case, when the charge was withdrawn, received a life pension on leaving the Bastille. At other times, the detention of an individual might throw his family into want. He was kept in the Bastille, if it was thought he deserved it, but his people were assisted. Under date September 3, 1763, the Duke de Choiseul writes to the lieutenant of police : " I have received the letter you did me the honour of writing to me in favour of the children of the Sieur Joncaire-Chabert. I have the pleasure to inform you that I have got for them a second subsidy of 300 livres (nearly £30 to-day) in consideration of the sad condition you informed me they were in." Louis XIV. guaranteed to Pellisson, at his liberation, a pension of 2000 crowns. The Regent granted to Voltaire, when he left the Bastille, a pension of 1200 livres. Louis XVI. awarded to Latude an annuity of 400 livres, and to La Rocheguérault an annuity of 400 crowns. The minister Breteuil pensioned all the prisoners whom he set at liberty. Brun de Condamine, confined from 1779 to 1783, received on leaving a sum of 600 livres. Renneville speaks of a prisoner to whom Seignelay gave an important situation in compensation for his detention at the Bastille. We hear of one, Toussaint Socquart, a commissioner of the Châtelet and of police, whose offices were restored to him when he came out of the Bastille. In fact, contrary to detention in our modern prisons, incarceration in the Bastille did not cast the slightest slur on the prisoner's character, even in the eyes of those to whom his arrest was due, and instances have been known of men who, on their release from the

Bastille, not only were reinstated in public offices, but reached the highest positions.

Until his examinations were quite completed, the prisoner was kept in close confinement. None but the officers of the château were allowed to communicate with him. And during this time he lived in solitude, unless he had brought a servant with him. The administration readily permitted the prisoners to avail themselves of the services of their valets, who were boarded at the king's expense. It even happened that the government sometimes gave their prisoners valets, paying not only for their board, but also their wages at the rate of 900 livres a year. One might cite prisoners of inferior rank who thus had servants to wait on them. Two or three prisoners were sometimes put together in one room. Prison life has no greater terror than solitude. In absolute solitude many of the prisoners became mad. In company, the hours of captivity seemed less tedious and oppressive. Father and son, mother and daughter, aunt and niece, lived together. Many might be named. On September 7, 1693, a lady named De la Fontaine was taken to the Bastille for the second time. The first time, she had been imprisoned quite alone ; but this new detention evoked the compassion of the lieutenant of police, who, to please the poor lady, sent her husband to the Bastille, locked him up with her, and gave them a lackey to wait on them.

The examinations being ended, the prisoners enjoyed a greater liberty. They could then enter into communication with the people of the town. They obtained permission to see their relatives and friends. These sometimes paid them visits in their rooms; but as a rule the interviews took place in the council-hall, in presence of one of the officers of the château. They were usually permitted to discuss only family affairs and business matters. All conversation on the Bastille and the reasons for their imprisonment was forbidden. The rules of the prison increased in severity as time went on. Towards the end of Louis XV.'s reign the lieutenant of police went so far as to prescribe the subjects of conversation which would alone be permitted in the course of the visits the prisoners received. "They may talk to the prisoner about the harvest his vineyards will yield this year, about cancelling a lease, about a match for his niece, about the health of his parents." But it is necessary to read the *Memoirs* of Gourville, Fontaine, Bussy-Rabutin, Hennequin, Madame de Staal, the Duke de Richelieu, to form a general idea of life at the Bastille under Louis XIV. and under the Regent. Several prisoners were free to move about through the château wherever it seemed good to them; they entered the rooms of their fellow-prisoners at all hours of the day. The governor contented himself with locking them in their own rooms at night. The prisoners who had the "liberty of the court" organized games of bowls or *tonneau*, and hobnobbed with the officers of the garrison. Fontaine relates that they might have been seen from the top of the towers, collected fifty at a time in the inner court

Bussy-Rabutin's room was open to all comers: his wife and friends visited him; he gave dinners to persons from court, plotted love intrigues there, and corresponded freely with his friends and relatives. Several prisoners even had permission to take a walk into the town on condition of their returning to the château in the evening. Two brothers were placed in the Bastille together. They went out when they pleased, taking turns; it was sufficient for one or other to be always at the château. The officers of the staff gossiped with the prisoners and gave them advice as to the best means of obtaining their liberty.

This animated, courtly, and elegant life is described with infinite charm by Madame de Staal, whom we have already cited. "We all used to spend a part of the day with the governor. We dined with him, and after dinner I enjoyed a rubber of ombre with Messieurs de Pompadour and de Boisdavis, Ménil advising me. When it was over we returned to our own apartments. The company met again in my rooms before supper, for which we returned to the governor's, and after that we all went to bed."

As to the manner in which the prisoners were fed and looked after, that is surprising indeed, and what we shall say about it, though rigidly accurate, will perhaps be regarded as an exaggeration. The governor drew three livres a day for the maintenance of a man of inferior rank; five livres for the maintenance of a tradesman; ten livres for a banker, a magistrate, or a man of letters; fifteen livres for a judge of the Parlement; thirty-six livres for a marshal of France. The Cardinal de Rohan had 120 francs a day spent on him. The Prince de Courlande, during a stay of five months at the Bastille, spent 22,000 francs. These figures must be doubled and trebled to give the value they would represent to-day.

We read, too, with the greatest astonishment the description of the meals the prisoners made. Renneville, whose evidence is the more important in that his book is a pamphlet against the administration of the Bastille, speaks in these terms of his first meal: "The turnkey put one of my serviettes on the table and placed my dinner on it, which consisted of pea soup garnished with lettuce, well simmered and appetizing to look at, with a quarter of fowl to follow; in one dish there was a juicy beef-steak, with plenty of gravy and a sprinkling of parsley, in another a quarter of forcemeat pie well stuffed with sweetbreads, cock's combs, asparagus, mushrooms, and truffles; and in a third a ragoût of sheep's tongue, the whole excellently cooked; for dessert, a biscuit and two pippins. The turnkey insisted on pouring out my wine. This was good burgundy, and the bread was excellent. I asked him to drink, but he declared it was not permitted. I asked if I should pay for my food, or whether I was indebted to the king for it. He told me that I had only to ask freely for whatever would give me pleasure, that they would try to satisfy me, and that His Majesty paid for it all." The "most Christian" king desired that his guests should fast on Fridays and in Lent, but he did not treat them any the worse on that account. "I had," says Renneville, "six dishes, and an admirable prawn soup. Among the fish there was a very fine weever, a large fried sole, and a perch, all very well seasoned, with three other dishes." At this period Renneville's board cost ten francs a day; later he was reduced to the rate of the prisoners of a lower class. "They much reduced my usual fare," he says; "I had, however, a good soup with fried bread crumbs, a passable piece of beef, a ragoût of sheep's tongue, and two custards for dessert. I was treated in pretty much the same manner the whole time I was in this gloomy place; sometimes they gave me, after my soup, a wing or leg of fowl, sometimes they put two little patties on the edge of the dish."

Towards the end of Louis XV.'s reign, Dumouriez eulogizes the cookery of the Bastille in almost the same temrs. On the day of his entrance, noticing that they were serving a fish dinner, he asked for a fowl to be got from a neighbouring eating-house. "A fowl!" said the major, "don't you know that to-day is Friday?" "Your business is to look after me and not my conscience. I am an invalid, for the Bastille itself is a disease," replied the prisoner. In an hour's time the fowl was on the table. Subsequently he asked for his dinner and supper to be served at the same time, between three and four o'clock. His valet, a good cook, used to make him stews. "You fared very well at the Bastille;

there were always five dishes at dinner and three at supper, without the dessert, and the whole being put on the table at once, appeared magnificent." There is a letter from the major of the Bastille addressed in 1764 to the lieutenant of police, discussing a prisoner named Vieilh, who never ate butcher's meat ; so they had to feed him exclusively on game and poultry. Things were much the same under Louis XVI., as Poultier d'Elmotte testifies : " De Launey, the governor, used to come and have a friendly chat with me ; he got them to consult my taste as regards food, and to supply me with anything I wished for." The bookseller Hardy, transferred in 1766 to the Bastille with the members of the Breton deputation, declares frankly that they were all treated in the best possible way. Finally, Linguet himself, in spite of his desire to paint the lot of the victims of the Bastille in the most sombre colours, is obliged to confess that food was supplied in abundance. Every morning the cook sent up to him a menu on which he marked the dishes he fancied.

The account books of the Bastille confirm the testimony of former prisoners. The following, according to these documents, are the meals that La Bourdonnais enjoyed during July, 1750. Every day the menu contains soup, beef, veal, beans, French beans, two eggs, bread, strawberries, cherries, gooseberries, oranges, two bottles of red wine, and two bottles of beer. In addition to this regular bill of fare we note on July 2, a fowl and a bottle of Muscat ; on the 4th, a bottle of Muscat ; on the 7th, tea;

on the 12th, a bottle of brandy; on the 13th, some flowers; on the 14th, some quails; on the 15th, a turkey; on the 16th, a melon; on the 17th, a fowl; on the 18th, a young rabbit; on the 19th, a bottle of brandy; on the 20th, a chicken and ham sausage and two melons; and so on.

Tavernier was a prisoner of mean station, son of a doorkeeper of Pâris de Montmartel. He was implicated in a plot against the King's life, and was one of the seven prisoners set free on the 14th of July. He was found out of his mind in his cell. After he had been led in triumph through the streets of Paris, he was shut up at Charenton. He was a martyr, people exclaimed. He was certainly not so well off in his new abode as he had been at the Bastille. We have an account of what was supplied to him at the Bastille in addition to the ordinary meals, in November, 1788, in March and May, 1789, three of the last months of his imprisonment. In November we find: tobacco, four bottles of brandy, sixty bottles of wine, thirty bottles of beer, two pounds of coffee, three pounds of sugar, a turkey, oysters, chestnuts, apples, and pears; in March: tobacco, four bottles of brandy, forty-four bottles of wine, sixty bottles of beer, coffee, sugar, fowls, cheese; in May: tobacco, four bottles of brandy, sixty-two bottles of wine, thirty-one bottles of beer, pigeons, coffee, sugar, cheese, &c. We have the menus of the Marquis de Sade for January, 1789: chocolate cream, a fat chicken stuffed with chestnuts, pullets with truffles, potted ham, apricot marmalade, &c.

Life in the Bastille

The facts we are describing were the rule. The prisoners who were treated with the least consideration fed very well. Only those who were sent down to the cells were sometimes put on bread and water, but that was only a temporary punishment.

When a complaint was formulated by any prisoner in regard to his food, a reprimand to the governor soon followed. Then the lieutenant of police inquired of the person concerned if he was better treated than formerly. "His Majesty tells me," writes Pontchartrain to De Launey, "that complaints have been raised about the bad food of the prisoners; he instructs me to write to you to give the matter great attention." And Sartine wrote jokingly to Major de Losmes : " I am quite willing for you to get the clothes of Sieur Dubois enlarged, and I hope all your prisoners may enjoy as excellent health."

Further, the king clothed those of the prisoners who were too poor to buy their own clothes. He did not give them a prison uniform, but dressing-gowns padded or lined with rabbit skin, breeches of coloured stuff, vests lined with silk plush and fancy coats.[1] The commissary at the Bastille appointed to look after the supplies took the prisoners' measure, and inquired about their

---

[1] "1751, March 2. I have received a letter from Dr. Duval (secretary to the lieutenant of police), in which he tells me that M. Berryer (lieutenant of police) is struck with the cost of the clothes supplied to the prisoners for some time past ; but, as you know, I only supply things when ordered by M. Berryer, and I try to supply good clothes, so that they may last and give the prisoners satisfaction."—Letter from Rochebrune, commissary to the Bastille, to Major Chevalier.

tastes, and the colours and styles that suited them best. A lady prisoner named Sauvé asked to have made for her a dress of white silk, dotted with green flowers. The wife of commissary Rochebrune spent several days in going the round of the Paris shops, and then wrote in despair that no dressmaker had such a material, the nearest approach to it being a white silk with green stripes: if Madame Sauvé would be satisfied with that, they would send to take her measure. "Monsieur le major," writes a prisoner named Hugonnet, "the shirts they brought me yesterday are not a bit what I asked for, for I remember having written 'fine, and with embroidered ruffles'; instead of which these things are coarse, made of wretched linen, and with ruffles at best only fit for a turnkey; and so I shall be glad if you will send them back to the commissary; and let him keep them, for I declare I won't have them."

The governor also saw that the prisoners had some means of diversion. The poorest he provided with pocket-money and tobacco.

About the beginning of the seventeenth century, a Neapolitan named Vinache died at the Bastille, after founding a library there for the use of his fellow-prisoners. This library was gradually augmented by donations from the governors, by gifts from various prisoners, and even by the generosity of a citizen of Paris whose compassion had been excited for the lot of the prisoners. The books consisted of romances, works of science and philosophy, and religious books, light literature pre-

LIFE IN THE BASTILLE

dominating. The lieutenant of police, Berryer, struck out of the list of books that were being sent one day to the binder a "poem on the greatness of God," as being on "too melancholy a subject for prisoners." The prisoners also procured books from outside. We have mentioned the Comte de Belle-Isle, who had more than three hundred books and atlases at the Bastille. La Beaumelle collected a library of more than 600 volumes. The administration, moreover, never refused to get for the prisoners, out of the royal funds and sometimes at considerable expense, such works as they said were necessary to their studies. The works of Voltaire and Puffendorf were readily placed in their hands. Finally, under Louis XVI., they were allowed to read the gazettes.

After the permission to have books and to write, the most coveted favour was that of walking exercise. Refusal of this was rare. The prisoners might walk, either on the towers of the Bastille, or in the inner courts, or lastly along the bastion, which was transformed into a garden. To fresh invigorating air the platform of the towers added the attraction of the finest view. Fontaine relates that Sacy went to the top of the towers every day after dinner. He there walked about in company with the officers, who gave him news of the town and the prisoners.

In their rooms the prisoners amused themselves with feeding cats and birds and animals of all kinds: they taught dogs tricks. Some were allowed to have a violin or a clavecin. Pellisson was shut up with a Basque who used to play to him on the musette. The Duke de Richelieu boasts of the operatic airs he sang in parts with his neighbours in the Bastille, Mdlle. de Launay among them, with her head at the bars of her window; "we got up choruses of a sort, with fine effect."

Other prisoners killed time with embroidery, weaving or knitting; some made ornaments for the chapel of the château. Some devoted themselves to carpentry, turned wood, made small articles of furniture. Artists painted and sketched. "The occupation of M. de Villeroi was somewhat singular: he had very fine clothes, which he was for ever unpicking and sewing together again with much cleverness." The prisoners who lived several in one room played at cards, chess, and backgammon. In 1788, at the time of the troubles in Brittany, a dozen noblemen of that country were shut up in the Bastille. They lived together, and asked for a billiard table to amuse themselves; the table was set up in the apartments of the major, and there these gentlemen went for their games.

The prisoners who died in the Bastille were interred in the graveyard of St. Paul's; the funeral service was held in the church of St. Paul, and the burial certificate, bearing the family name of the deceased, was drawn up in the vestry. It is not true that the names of the deceased were wrongly stated in the register in order that their identity might be concealed from the public. The Man in the Iron Mask was inscribed on the register of St. Paul's under his real name. Jews, Protestants, and suicides were buried in the garden of the château, the prejudices of the period not allowing their remains to be laid in consecrated ground.

Those who were liberated had a happier fate. Their dismissal was ordered by a *lettre de cachet*, as their incarceration had been. These orders for their liberation, so anxiously expected, were brought by the court " distributors of packets " or by the ordinary post ; sometimes relatives and friends themselves brought the sealed envelope, in order to have the joy of taking away at once those whose deliverance they came to effect.

The governor, or, in his absence, the king's lieutenant, came into the prisoner's chamber and announced that he was free. The papers and other effects which had been taken from him on entrance were restored to him, the major getting a receipt for them ; then he signed a promise to reveal nothing of what he had seen at the château. Many of the prisoners refused to submit to this formality, and were liberated notwithstanding ; others, after having signed, retailed everywhere all they knew about the prison, and were not interfered with. When the prisoner only recovered his freedom under certain conditions, he was required to give an undertaking to submit to the king's pleasure.

All these formalities having been completed, the governor, with that feeling for good form which characterized the men of the *ancien régime*, had the man who had been his guest served for the last time with an excellent dinner. If the prisoner was a man of good society, the governor would even go so far as to invite him to his own table, and then, the meal over and the good-byes said, he placed his own carriage at the prisoner's disposal, and often entered it himself to accompany him to his destination.

More than one prisoner thus restored to the world must have felt greatly embarrassed before a day was past, and have been at a loss what to do or where to go. The administration of the Bastille sometimes gave money to one and another to enable them to get along for a time. In December, 1783, a certain Dubu de la Tagnerette, after being set at liberty, was lodged in the governor's house for a fortnight until he had found apartments that would suit him. Moreover, many of the prisoners were actually annoyed at being dismissed: we could cite examples of persons who sought to get themselves sent to the Bastille; others refused to accept their liberty, and others did their best to get their detention prolonged.

"Many come out," says Renneville "very sad at having to leave." Le Maistre de Sacy and Fontaine affirm that the years spent at the Bastille were the best years in their lives. "The innocent life we lived," says Renneville again, "Messieurs Hamilton, Schrader, and myself, seemed so pleasant to M. Hamilton that he begged me to write a description of it in verse." The *Memoirs* of Madame de Staal represent her years at the Bastille as the happiest she ever knew. "In my heart of hearts, I was very far from desiring my liberty."

"I stayed at the Bastille for six weeks," observes the Abbé Morellet, "which sped away—I chuckle still as I think of them—very pleasantly for me." And later, Dumouriez declares that at the Bastille he was happy and never felt dull.

Such was the rule of the celebrated state prison. In the last century there was no place of detention in Europe where the prisoners were surrounded with so many comforts and attentions: there is no such place in these days.

But in spite of these very real alleviations, it would be absurd to pretend that the prisoners were in general reconciled to their incarceration. Nothing is a consolation for the loss of liberty. How many poor wretches, in their despair, have dashed their heads against the thick walls while wife and children and concerns of the utmost gravity were summoning them from without! The Bastille was the cause of ruin to many; within its walls were shed tears which were never dried.

An eighteenth-century writer thus defined the state prison: "A bastille is any house solidly built, hermetically sealed, and diligently guarded, where any person, of whatever rank, age, or sex, may enter without knowing why, remain without knowing how long, hoping to leave it, but not knowing how." These lines, written by an apologist for the old state prison, contain its condemnation, without appeal, before the modern mind.

CHAPTER IV.

THE MAN IN THE IRON MASK.

FOR two centuries no question has excited public opinion more than that of the Man in the Iron Mask. The books written on the subject would fill a library. People despaired of ever lifting the veil. "The story of the Iron Mask," says Michelet, "will probably remain for ever obscure," and Henri Martin adds: "History has no right to pronounce judgment on what will never leave the domain of conjecture." To-day, the doubt no longer exists. The problem is solved. Before disclosing the solution which criticism has unanimously declared correct, we propose to transcribe the scanty authentic documents that we possess on the masked man, and then to state the principal solutions which have been proposed, before arriving at the true solution.

1. THE DOCUMENTS.

The Register of the Bastille.—To begin with, let us quote the text which is the origin and foundation of all the works published on the question of the Iron Mask.

Etienne du Junca, king's lieutenant at the Bastille,

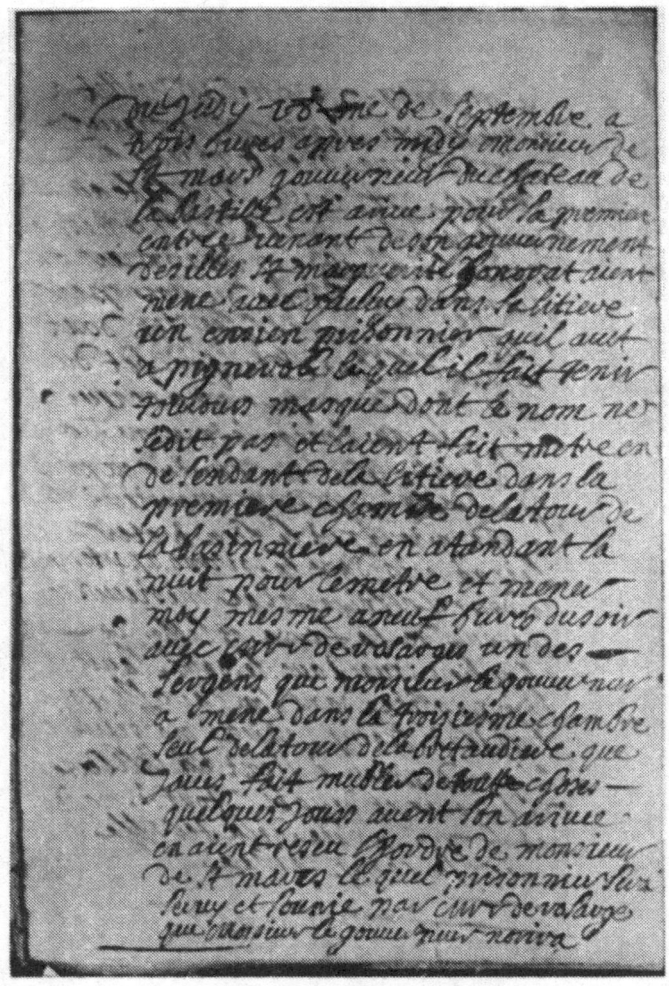

Note in Du Junca's Journal regarding the entrance to the Bastille (September 18, 1698) of the Man in the Iron Mask.

in a journal which he began to keep on October 2, 1690, when he entered upon his office—a sort of register in which he recorded day by day the details concerning the arrival of the prisoners—writes, under date September 18, 1698, these lines,[1] which the popular legend has rendered memorable :—

"Thursday, September 18 (1698), at three o'clock in the afternoon, M. de Saint-Mars, governor of the château of the Bastille, made his first appearance, coming from his governorship of the Isles of Sainte-Marguerite-Honorat, bringing with him, in his conveyance, a prisoner he had formerly at Pignerol, whom he caused to be always masked, whose name is not mentioned; directly he got out of the carriage he put him in the first room of the Bazinière tower, waiting till night for me to take him, at nine o'clock, and put him with M. de Rosarges, one of the sergeants brought by the governor, alone in the third room of the Bertaudière tower, which I had had furnished with all necessaries some days before his arrival, having received orders to that effect from M. de Saint-Mars: the which prisoner will be looked after and waited on by M. de Rosarges, and maintained by the governor."

In a second register, supplementary to the first, in which du Junca records details of the liberation or the death of the prisoners, we read, under date November 19, 1703 :—

---

[1] These extracts are translated literally, in order to preserve the clumsy constructions of the unlettered official.—T.

"On the same day, November 19, 1703, the unknown prisoner, always masked with a mask of black velvet, whom M. de Saint-Mars, the governor, brought with him on coming from the Isles de Sainte-Marguerite, whom he had kept for a long time, the which happening to be a little ill yesterday on coming from mass, he died to-day, about ten o'clock at night, without having had a serious illness; it could not have been slighter. M. Giraut, our chaplain, confessed him yesterday, is surprised at his death. He did not receive the sacrament, and our chaplain exhorted him a moment before he died. And this unknown prisoner, kept here for so long, was buried on Tuesday at four o'clock p.m., November 20, in the graveyard of St. Paul, our parish; on the register of burial he was given a name also unknown. M. de Rosarges, major, and Arreil, surgeon, signed the register."

And in the margin :—

"I have since learnt that they called him M. de Marchiel on the register, and that forty livres was the cost of the funeral."

The registers of du Junca were preserved among the ancient archives of the Bastille, whence they passed to the Arsenal library, where they are now kept. They are drawn up in the clumsy handwriting of a soldier, with little skill in penmanship. The spelling is bad. But the facts are stated with precision, and have always proved accurate when checked.

The extract from the second register shows that the

Du mesme jour lundy 19 ma de
novembre 1703 — le prisonnier
Inconeu toujours masqué, d'un masque
de velours noir, que Monsieur de
St Mars gouverneur a mené avec
que luy en venant des Illes St margueritte
quil gardoit depuis longtamps, lequel
s'etant trouvé hier un peu mal en
sortant de la messe il est mort
se jourduy sur les dix heures du
soir sans avoir eu une grande
maladie il ne seput pas moins
mr girault nottre aumonier le
comfessa hier sur pris de la mort
il n'apoint receu les sacremens
et nottre aumonier l'a exorté un
momant avend que de mourir
et se prisonnier Inconeu gardé de
puis silontamps a esté entere
le mardy a quattre heures de la
pres midy 20 me novembre dans
le semetiere St paul nottre p...
+ de apris du voisse eu sur le registre mortuel +
depuis constant on donne un nom aussy Inconeu
nomé sur le registre que Monsieur de Rosarges maior
ont demarvesfille
que onapaié — tur veil sieurgien qui sont
40 m deniers
mant signé sur le registre

Notice in Du Junca's Journal of the death of the masked prisoner in the Bastille (November 19, 1703).

mysterious prisoner wore, not a mask of iron, but one of black velvet.

Further, the entry on the register of St. Paul's church has been discovered. It reads :—

"On the 19th, Marchioly, aged 45 years or thereabouts, died in the Bastille, whose body was buried in the churchyard of St. Paul, his parish, the 20th of the present month, in the presence of M. Rosage (*sic*), major of the Bastille, and of M. Reglhe (*sic*), surgeon major of the Bastille, who signed.—(Signed) ROSARGES, REILHE."

Such are the fundamental documents for the story of the Iron Mask; we shall see by and by that they are sufficient to establish the truth.

The Letter of the Governor of Sainte-Marguerite.—We have just seen, from the register of du Junca, that the masked man had been at the Isles of Sainte-Marguerite under the charge of Saint-Mars, who, on being appointed governor of the Bastille, had brought the prisoner with him. In the correspondence exchanged between Saint-Mars and the minister Barbezieux, occurs the following letter, dated January 6, 1696, in which Saint-Mars describes his method of dealing with the prisoners, and the masked man is referred to under the appellation "my ancient prisoner."

"MY LORD,—You command me to tell you what is the practice, when I am absent or ill, as to the visits made and precautions taken daily in regard to the prisoners committed to my charge. My two lieutenants serve the meals at the regular hours, just as they have seen me do, and as I still do very often when I am well. The first of my lieutenants, who takes the keys of the prison of *my ancient prisoner*, with whom we commence, opens the three doors and enters the chamber of the prisoner, who politely hands him the plates and dishes, put one on top of another, to give them into the hands of the lieutenant, who has only to go through two doors to hand them to one of my sergeants, who takes them and places them on a table two steps away, where is the second lieutenant, who examines everything that enters and leaves the prison, and sees that there is nothing written on the plate ; and after they have given him the utensil, they examine his bed inside and out, and then the gratings and windows of his room, and very often the man himself : after having asked him very politely if he wants anything else, they lock the doors and proceed to similar business with the other prisoners."

The Letter of M. de Palteau.—On June 19, 1768, M. de Formanoir de Palteau addressed from the château of Palteau, near Villeneuve-le-Roi, to the celebrated Fréron, editor of the *Année Littéraire*, a letter which was inserted in the number for June 30, 1768. The author of this letter was the grand-nephew of Saint-Mars. At the time when the latter was appointed governor of the Bastille, the château of Palteau belonged to him, and he halted there with his prisoner on the way from the Isles of Sainte-Marguerite to Paris.

"In 1698," writes M. de Palteau, "M. de Saint-Mars passed from the governorship of the Isles of Sainte-Marguerite to that of the Bastille. On his way to take up his duties, he stayed with his prisoner on his estate at Palteau. The masked man arrived in a conveyance which preceded that of M. de Saint-Mars; they were accompanied by several horsemen. The peasants went to meet their lord: M. de Saint-Mars ate with his prisoner, who had his back turned to the windows of the dining-hall looking on the courtyard. The peasants whom I have questioned could not see whether he ate with his mask on; but they observed very well that M. de Saint-Mars, who was opposite him at table, had two pistols beside his plate. They had only one footman to wait on them, and he fetched the dishes from an ante-room where they were brought him, carefully shutting the door of the dining-hall behind him. When the prisoner crossed the courtyard, he always had his black mask over his face; the peasants noticed that his lips and teeth were not covered, that he was tall and had white hair. M. de Saint-Mars slept in a bed that was put up for him near that of the masked man."

This account is marked throughout with the stamp of truth. M. de Palteau, the writer, makes no attempt to draw inferences from it. He declares for none of the hypotheses then under discussion in regard to the identity of the mysterious unknown. He is content to report the testimony of those of his peasants who saw the masked man when he passed through their lord's estates.

The only detail in the story which we are able to check—a characteristic detail, it is true—is that of the black mask of which M. de Palteau speaks: it corresponds exactly to the mask of black velvet mentioned in du Junca's register.

The château of Palteau is still in existence. In his work on Superintendent Fouquet, M. Jules Lair gives a description of it. "The château of Palteau, situated on an eminence among woods and vines, presented at that time, as it does to-day, the aspect of a great lordly mansion in the style of the time of Henri IV. and Louis XIII. First there is a wide courtyard, then two wings; within, the principal building and the chapel. The lower story is supported on arches, and its lofty windows go right up into the roof, and light the place from floor to attic." Since the eighteenth century, however, the château has undergone some modifications. The room in which Saint-Mars dined with his prisoner is now used as a kitchen.

The Notes of Major Chevalier.—In addition to the entries in du Junca's Journal which we have transcribed, scholars are accustomed to invoke, as equally worthy of credence though later in date, the testimony of Father Griffet, chaplain of the Bastille, and that of Major Chevalier.

The extracts from du Junca quoted above were published for the first time in 1769 by Father Griffet, who added the following comments: "The memory of the masked prisoner was still preserved among the officers, soldiers, and servants of the Bastille, when M. de Launey, who has long been the governor, came to occupy a place on the staff of the garrison. Those who had seen him with his mask, when he crossed the courtyard on his way to attend mass, said that after his death the order was given to burn everything he had used, such as linen, clothes, cushions, counterpanes, &c.: that the very walls of the room he had occupied had to be scraped and whitewashed again, and that all the tiles of the flooring were taken up and replaced by others, because they were so afraid that he had found the means to conceal some notes or some mark, the discovery of which would have revealed his name."

The testimony of Father Griffet happens to be confirmed by some notes from the pen of a major of the Bastille named Chevalier. The major was not a personage of the highest rank in the administration of the Bastille, since above him were the governor and the king's lieutenant: but he was the most important personage. The whole internal administration, so far as the prisoners were concerned, was entrusted to him. Chevalier fulfilled these duties for nearly thirty-eight years, from 1749 to 1787. M. Fernand Bournon's estimate of him is as follows: "Chevalier is a type of the devoted hard-working official who has no ambition to rise above a rather subordinate rank. It would be impossible to say how much the administration of the Bastille owed to his zeal and to his perfect familiarity with a service of extraordinary difficulty."

Among notes put together with a view to a history of the Bastille, Chevalier gives in condensed form the information furnished by du Junca's register, and adds: " This is the famous masked man whom no one has ever known. He was treated with great distinction by the governor, and was seen only by M. de Rosarges, major of the said château, who had sole charge of him ; he was not ill except for a few hours, and died rather suddenly : interred at St. Paul's, on Tuesday, November 20, 1703, at 4 o'clock p.m., under the name of Marchiergues. He was buried in a new white shroud, given by the governor, and practically everything in his room was burnt, such as his bed, chairs, tables, and other bits of furniture, or else melted down, and the whole was thrown into the privies."

These notes of Father Griffet and Major Chevalier have derived great force, in the eyes of historians, from their exact agreement ; but a close examination shows that the testimony of Chevalier was the source of Father Griffet's information ; in fact, Chevalier was major of the Bastille when the Jesuit compiled his work, and it is doubtless upon his authority that the latter depended.

Documents recently published in the *Revue Bleue* upset these assertions, which appeared to be based on the firmest foundations.

In the Journal of du Junca, which we have already mentioned, we read under date April 30, 1701 : "Sunday, April 30, about 9 o'clock in the evening, M. Aumont the younger came, bringing and handing over to us a prisoner named M. Maranville, alias Ricarville, who was an officer in the army, a malcontent, too free with his tongue, a worthless fellow : whom I received in obedience to the king's orders sent through the Count of Pontchartrain : whom I have had put along with the man Tirmon, in the second room of the Bertaudière tower, with the *ancient prisoner*, both being well locked in."

The "ancient prisoner" here referred to is no other than the masked man. When he entered the Bastille, as we have seen, on September 18, 1698, he was placed in the third room of the Bertaudière tower. In 1701, the Bastille happened to be crowded with prisoners, and they had to put several together in one and the same room; so the man in the mask was placed with two companions. One of them, Jean-Alexandre de Ricarville, also called Maranville, had been denounced as a "retailer of ill speech against the State, finding fault with the policy of France and lauding that of foreigners, especially that of the Dutch." The police reports depict him as a beggarly fellow, poorly dressed, and about sixty years old. He had formerly been, as du Junca says, an officer in the royal troops. Maranville left the Bastille on October 19, 1708. He was transferred to Charenton, where he died in February, 1709. It must be pointed out that Charenton was then an "open" prison, where the prisoners associated with one another and had numerous relations with the outside world.

The second of the fellow-prisoners of the man in the mask, Dominique-François Tirmont, was a servant.

When he was placed in the Bastille, on July 30, 1700, he was nineteen years old. He was accused of sorcery and of debauching young girls. He was put in the second room of the Bertaudière tower, where he was joined by Maranville and the man in the mask. On December 14, 1701, he was transferred to Bicêtre. He lost his reason in 1703 and died in 1708.

The man in the mask was taken out of the third room of the Bertaudière tower, in which he had been placed on his entrance to the Bastille, on March 6, 1701, in order to make room for a woman named Anne Randon, a "witch and fortune-teller," who was shut up alone in it. The masked prisoner was then placed in the "second Bertaudière" with Tirmont, who had been there, as we have just seen, since July 30, 1700. Maranville joined them on April 30, 1701. Not long after, the masked man was transferred to another room, with or without Maranville. Tirmont had been taken to Bicêtre in 1701. We find that on February 26, 1703, the Abbé Gonzel, a priest of Franche-Comté, accused of being a spy, was shut up alone in the "second Bertaudière."

These facts are of undeniable authenticity, and one sees at a glance the consequences springing from them. At the time when the masked prisoner shared the same room with fellow-captives, other prisoners at the Bastille were kept rigorously isolated, in spite of the crowded state of the prison, so much more important did the reasons for their incarceration seem! The man in the mask was associated with persons of the lowest class, who were soon afterwards to leave and take their places with the ruck of prisoners at Charenton and Bicêtre. We read in a report of D'Argenson that there was even some talk of enlisting one of them, Tirmont, in the army. Such, then, was this strange personage, the repository of a terrible secret of which Madame Palatine [1] was already speaking in mysterious terms, the man who puzzled kings, Louis XV., Louis XVI., who puzzled the very officers of the Bastille, and caused them to write stories as remote as possible from the reality!

2. THE LEGEND.

If the very officers of the Bastille indulged such wild freaks of imagination, what flights into dreamland might not the thoughts of the public be expected to take? The movement is a very curious one to follow. To begin with, we have the light Venetian mask transforming itself

[1] Step-sister of Louis XIV. The following extracts from her correspondence show how, even in circles that might have been expected to be well informed, the legend had already seized on people's imaginations:—

"Marly, October 10, 1711. A man remained long years in the Bastille, and has died there, masked. At his side he had two musketeers ready to kill him if he took off his mask. He ate and slept masked. No doubt there was some reason for this, for otherwise he was well treated and lodged, and given everything he wished for. He went to communion masked; he was very devout and read continually. No one has ever been able to learn who he was."

"Versailles, October 22, 1711. I have just learnt who the masked man was, who died in the Bastille. His wearing a mask was not due to cruelty. He was an English lord who had been mixed up in the affair of the Duke of Berwick (natural son of James II.) against King William. He died there so that the king might never know what became of him."

into an iron mask with steel articulations which the prisoner was never without. The consideration—imaginary, as we have seen—with which the prisoner is supposed to have been treated, and which is referred to in the notes of Major Chevalier, becomes transformed into marks of a boundless deference shown by the jailers towards their captive. The story was that Saint-Mars, the governor, a knight of St. Louis, never spoke to the prisoner except standing, with bared head, that he served him at table with his own hands and on silver plate, and that he supplied him with the most luxurious raiment his fancy could devise. Chevalier says that after his death his room at the Bastille was done up like new, to prevent his successor from discovering any tell-tale evidence in some corner. Speaking of the time when the masked man was at the Isles of Sainte-Marguerite, Voltaire relates: "One day the prisoner wrote with a knife on a silver dish, and threw the dish out of the window towards a boat moored on the shore, almost at the foot of the tower. A fisherman, to whom the boat belonged, picked up the dish and carried it to the governor. Astonished, he asked the fisherman, 'Have you read what is written on this dish, and has anyone seen it in your hands?' 'I cannot read,' replied the fisher, 'I have only just found it, and no one has seen it.' The poor man was detained until the governor was assured he could not read and that no one had seen the dish. 'Go,' he said, 'it is lucky for you that you can't read!'"

In Father Papon's *History of Provence*, linen takes the place of the dish. The upshot is more tragic: "I found in the citadel an officer of the Free Company, aged 79 years. He told me several times that a barber of that company saw one day, under the prisoner's window, something white floating on the water; he went and picked it up and carried it to M. de Saint Mars. It was a shirt of fine linen, folded with no apparent care, and covered with the prisoner's writing. M. de Saint-Mars, after unfolding it and reading a few lines, asked the barber, with an air of great embarrassment, if he had not had the curiosity to read what was on it. The barber protested over and over again that he had read nothing; but, two days after, he was found dead in his bed."

And the fact that Saint-Mars had had the body of the prisoner buried in a white cloth struck the imagination, and was developed in its turn into an extraordinary taste on the part of the prisoner for linen of the finest quality and for costly lace—all which was taken to prove that the masked man was a son of Anne of Austria, who had a very special love, it was declared, for valuable lace and fine linen.

A Brother of Louis XIV.—We are able to fix with precision, we believe, the origin of the legend which made the Iron Mask a brother of Louis XIV. Moreover, it was due to this suggestion, which was hinted at from the first, that the story of the prisoner made so great a noise. The glory of it belongs to the most famous writer of the eighteenth century. With a boldness of imagination for which to-day he would be envied by the cleverest journalistic inventor of sensational paragraphs, Voltaire started this monstrous hoax on its vigorous flight.

In 1745 there had just appeared a sort of romance entitled *Notes towards the History of Persia*, which was attributed, not without some reason, to Madame de Vieux-Maisons. The book contained a story within a story, in which the mysterious prisoner, who was beginning to be talked about everywhere, was identified with the Duke de Vermandois, and to this fact was due the sensation which the book caused. Voltaire immediately saw how he could turn the circumstance to account. He had himself at one time been confined in the Bastille, which was one reason for speaking of it; but he did not dare put in circulation suddenly, without some preparation, the terrible story he had just conceived, and, with a very delicate sensitiveness to public opinion, he contented himself with printing the following paragraph in the first edition of his *Age of Louis XIV.*: "A few months after the death of Mazarin there occurred an event which is unexampled in history, and, what is not less strange, has been passed over in silence by all the historians. There was sent with the utmost secrecy to the château of the Isle of Sainte-Marguerite, in the Sea of Provence, an unknown prisoner, of more than ordinary height, young, and with features of rare nobility and beauty. On the way, this prisoner wore a mask the chinpiece of which was fitted with springs of steel, which allowed him to eat freely with the mask covering his face. The order had been given to kill him if he uncovered. He remained in the island until an officer in whom great confidence was placed, named Saint-Mars, governor of Pignerol, having been made governor of the Bastille, came to the Isle of Sainte-Marguerite to fetch him, and conducted him to the Bastille, always masked. The Marquis de Louvois saw him in the island before his removal, and remained standing while he spoke to him, with a consideration savouring of respect." Voltaire, however, does not say who this extraordinary prisoner was. He observed the impression produced on the public by his story. Then he ventured more boldly, and in the first edition of his *Questions on the Encyclopædia* insinuated that the motive for covering the prisoner's face with a mask was fear lest some too striking likeness should be recognized. He still refrained from giving his name, but already everyone was on tiptoe with the expectation of startling news. At last, in the second edition of *Questions on the Encyclopædia*, Voltaire intrepidly added that the man in the mask was a uterine brother of Louis XIV., a son of Mazarin and Anne of Austria, and older than the king. We know what incomparable agitators of public opinion the Encyclopædists were.

Once hatched, the story was not long in producing a numerous progeny, which grew in their turn and became a monstrous brood.

We read in the *Memoirs* of the Duke de Richelieu, compiled by his secretary the Abbé Soulavie, that Mdlle. de Valois, the Regent's daughter and at this date the mistress of Richelieu, consented, at the instigation of the latter, to prostitute herself to her father—tradition has it that the Regent was enamoured of his daughter—in order to get sight of an account of the Iron Mask drawn up by Saint-Mars. According to this story, which the author of the *Memoirs* prints in its entirety, Louis XIV. was born at noon, and at half-past eight in the evening, while the king was at supper, the queen was brought to bed of a second son, who was put out of sight so as to avoid subsequent dissensions in the state.

The Baron de Gleichen goes still farther. He is at the pains to prove that it was the true heir to the throne who was put out of sight, to the profit of a child of the queen and the cardinal. Having became masters of the situation at the death of the king, they substituted their son for the Dauphin, the substitution being facilitated by a strong likeness between the children. One sees at a glance the consequences of this theory, which nullifies the legitimacy of the last Bourbons.

But the career of imagination was not yet to be checked. The legend came into full bloom under the first empire. Pamphlets then appeared in which the version of Baron de Gleichen was revived. Louis XIV. had been only a bastard, the son of foreigners; the lawful heir had been imprisoned at the Isles of Sainte-Marguerite, where he had married the daughter of one of his keepers. Of this marriage was born a child who, as soon as he was weaned, was sent to Corsica, and entrusted to a reliable person, as a child coming of "good stock," in Italian, *Buona-parte*.

Of that child the Emperor was the direct descendant. The right of Napoleon I. to the throne of France established by the Iron Mask !—there is a discovery which the great Dumas missed. But, incredible as it seems, there were men who actually took these fables seriously. In a Vendéan manifesto circulated among the Chouans,[1] in Nivose of the year ix,[2] we read: "It is not wise for the Royalist party to rely on the assurances given by some emissaries of Napoleon, that he seized the throne only to restore the Bourbons; everything proves that he only awaits the general pacification to declare himself, and that he means to base his right on the birth of the children of the Iron Mask!"

We shall not stay to refute the hypothesis which makes the Iron Mask a brother of Louis XIV. Marius Topin has already done so in the clearest possible manner. The notion, moreover, has long been abandoned. The last writers who adhered to it date from the revolutionary period.

The Successive Incarnations of the Iron Mask.—"Never has an Indian deity," says Paul de Saint-Victor, speaking of the Iron Mask, "undergone so many metempsychoses

[1] The insurgents who rose for the king against the Revolutionists in Brittany: see Balzac's famous novel. The movement smouldered for a great many years.—T.

[2] The Gregorian calendar was abolished by the National Convention in 1793, who decreed that September 22, 1792, should be regarded as the first day of a new era. The year was divided into twelve months, with names derived from natural phenomena. Nivose (snowy) was the fourth of these months. Thus, the period mentioned in the text includes from December 21, 1800, to January 19, 1801.—T.

and so many avatars." It would take too long merely to enumerate all the individuals with whom it has been attempted to identify the Iron Mask: even women have not escaped. We shall cite rapidly the theories which have found most credence amongst the public, or those which have been defended in the most serious works, in order to arrive finally at the identification—as will be seen, it is one of those proposed long ago—which is beyond doubt the true one.

The hypothesis which, after that of a brother of Louis XIV., has most powerfully excited public opinion, is that which made the mysterious unknown Louis, Comte de Vermandois, admiral of France, and son of the charming Louise de la Vallière. This was indeed the belief of Father Griffet, chaplain of the Bastille, and even of the officers of the staff. But the conjecture is disproved in a single line: "The Comte de Vermandois died at Courtrai, on November 18, 1683." A precisely similar fact refutes the theory identifying the Iron Mask with the Duke of Monmouth, the natural son of Charles II. and Lucy Walters. Monmouth perished on the scaffold in 1683. Lagrange-Chancel throws much ardour and talent into a defence of the theory which made the Iron Mask Francis of Vendôme, Duke de Beaufort, who, under the Fronde, was called "King of the Markets." The Duke de Beaufort died at the siege of Candia, June 25, 1669.

To Lagrange-Chancel succeeds the Chevalier de Taulès. "I have discovered the Man in the Mask," he cries, "and it is my duty to impart my discovery to

Europe and posterity!" This discovery brings forward one Avedick, an Armenian patriarch of Constantinople and Jerusalem, kidnapped in the East at the instigation of the Jesuits, and transported to France. Vergennes, on entering the ministry for foreign affairs, set investigations on foot. They confirmed the statement that Avedick had actually been arrested in the circumstances indicated, but after 1706; and so he could not be identified with the Iron Mask.

Such were the theories of the eighteenth century. We come now to those of our own time. Since mystery and sinister machinations were involved, the Jesuits could not be long left out of the business. We have just seen them at their tricks with the Armenian patriarch. People dreamt of an innocent youth thrown into a dungeon at their instigation for having written a couple of verses against them. But even this fancy was completely cast into the shade in a work published in 1885 under the pseudonym of "Ubalde," the author of which was unquestionably M. Anatole Loquin. This is his conclusion: "The more I reflect, the more I believe I recognize in the Man in the Iron Mask, without any elaborate theory, without prejudice on my part, no other than J. B. Poquelin de Molière." The Jesuits have got their revenge for *Tartufe*!

Let us come now to the conjectures which have almost hit the truth and have been defended by genuine scholars.

Superintendent Fouquet is the solution of the

bibliophile Jacob (Paul Lacroix). M. Lair has shown that Fouquet died at Pignerol, of a sort of apoplexy, on March 23, 1680, at the very moment when there was an idea at court of sending him to the waters at Bourbon, as a first step towards his final liberation.

François Ravaisson, the learned and charming keeper of the Arsenal library, whose work in classifying the archives of the Bastille we have had the honour to continue, believed for a moment that the celebrated prisoner might have been the young Count de Kéroualze who had fought at Candia under the orders of Admiral de Beaufort. Ravaisson put forth his theory with much hesitation, and as, in the sequel, he was himself led to abandon it, we need not dwell any longer upon it.

M. Loiseleur, in the course of his brilliant controversy with Marius Topin, suggested " an obscure spy arrested by Catinat in 1681," and his opponent refuted him in the most piquant manner by discovering Catinat in the very prisoner he was said to have arrested!

General Jung published a large volume in support of the claims of a certain Oldendorf, a native of Lorraine, a spy and poisoner, arrested on March 29, 1673, in a trap laid for him at one of the passages of the Somme. The theory was refuted by M. Loiseleur. As M. Lair pointed out, General Jung did not even succeed in proving that his nominee entered Pignerol, an essential condition to his being the Man in the Mask.

Baron Carutti urged the claims of a mad Jacobin, a prisoner at Pignerol whose name remains unknown;

but this Jacobin died at Pignerol towards the close of 1693.

The recent work of M. Emile Burgaud, written in collaboration with Commandant Bazeries, made a great sensation. He fixes on General Vivien Labbé de Bulonde, whom Louvois arrested for having shown dereliction of a general's duty before Coni. M. Geoffroy de Grandmaison published in the *Univers* of January 9, 1895, two receipts signed by General de Bulonde, one in 1699, when the masked man was in rigorous isolation at the Bastille, the other in 1705, when he had been dead for two years.

We come at last to the hypothesis which is the most probable of all—after the true hypothesis, of course. Eustache Dauger, whom M. Lair identifies with the masked prisoner, was a valet, who had been put into jail at Pignerol on July 28, 1669. But it must be noted that the masked prisoner was kept guarded in rigorous secrecy in the early days of his detention, as long as he was at Pignerol and the Isles of Sainte-Marguerite. Now, when Dauger went to Pignerol, his case seemed of such slight importance that Saint-Mars thought of making him into a servant for the other prisoners, and in fact, in 1675, Louvois gave him as a valet to Fouquet, who for some time past had seen the rigour of his confinement sensibly mitigated, receiving visits, walking freely in the courts and purlieus of the fortress, Dauger accompanying him. Further, we know that the masked man was transferred direct from Pignerol to the Isles of

Sainte-Marguerite, whilst Dauger was transferred in 1681 to Exiles, whence he only went to the Isles in 1687.

We now come to the correct solution.

3. MATTIOLI.

To Baron Heiss, once captain in the Alsace regiment, and one of the most distinguished bibliophiles of his time, belongs the honour of being the first, in a letter dated from Phalsbourg, June 28, 1770, and published by the *Journal encyclopédique*, to identify the masked prisoner with Count Mattioli, secretary of state to the Duke of Mantua. After him, Dutens, in 1783, in his *Intercepted Correspondence;* Baron de Chambrier, in 1795, in a Memoir presented to the Academy of Berlin; Roux-Fazillac, member of the Legislative Assembly and the Convention, in a remarkable work printed in 1801; then successively, Reth, Delort, Ellis, Carlo Botta, Armand Baschet, Marius Topin, Paul de Saint-Victor, and M. Gallien, in a series of publications more or less important, endeavoured to prove that the Man in the Mask was the Duke of Mantua's secretary of state. The scholars most intimate with the history of Louis XIV.'s government, Depping, Chéruel, Camille Rousset, have not hesitated to pronounce in favour of the same view; while against them, singlehanded like his D'Artagnan, Alexandre Dumas resisted the efforts of twenty scholars, and the *Vicomte de Bragelonne*—giving a new lease of life to the legend about the brother of Louis XIV., put in circulation by Voltaire, and reinforced by the Revolution—drove back into their dust among the archives the documents which students had exhumed.

We have no longer to deal with so formidable an adversary, and we hope that the following pages will not leave the shadow of a doubt.

We know how, under the influence of Louvois, the able and insinuating policy directed first by Mazarin, then by Lionne, gave way to a military diplomacy, blunt and aggressive. Louis XIV. was master of Pignerol, acquired in 1632. He was induced by Louvois to cast covetous glances at Casal. In possession of these two places, the French armies could not but dominate Upper Italy, and hold the court of Turin directly at their mercy. The throne of Mantua was then occupied by a young duke, Charles IV. of Gonzago, frivolous, happy-go-lucky, dissipating his wealth at Venice in fêtes and pleasures. In 1677 he had pledged to the Jews the crown revenues for several years. Charles IV. was also Marquis of Montferrat, of which Casal was the capital. Noting with watchful eye the frivolity and financial straits of the young prince, the court of Versailles conceived the bold scheme of buying Casal for hard cash.

At this date, one of the principal personages in Mantua was Count Hercules Antony Mattioli. He was born at Bologna on December 1, 1640, of a distinguished family. A brilliant student, he had barely passed his twentieth year when he was elected a professor at the University of Bologna. Afterwards he established himself at Mantua, where Charles III., whose confidence he had won, made him his secretary of state. Charles IV., continuing the favour of his father, not only maintained Mattioli in his office as minister of state, but appointed him an honorary senator, a dignity which was enhanced by the title of Count.

Louis XIV. was employing at the capital of the Venetian republic a keen-witted and enterprising ambassador, the Abbé d'Estrades. He saw through the ambitious and intriguing nature of Mattioli, and, towards the end of 1677, succeeded in winning over his support for the designs of the French court on Casal.

On January 12, 1678, Louis XIV. with his own hand wrote expressing his thanks to Mattioli, who by-and-by came to Paris. On December 8, the contract was signed, the Duke of Mantua receiving in exchange for Casal 100,000 crowns. In a private audience, Louis XIV. presented Mattioli with a costly diamond and paid him the sum of a hundred double louis.

Scarcely two months after Mattioli's journey to France, the courts of Vienna, Madrid, Turin, and the Venetian Republic were simultaneously informed of all that had taken place. In order to reap a double harvest of gold, Mattioli had cynically betrayed both his master Charles IV. and the King of France. Like a thunderbolt there came to Versailles the news of the arrest of Baron d'Asfeld, the envoy appointed by Louis XIV. to exchange ratifications with Mattioli. The governor of Milan had caused him to be seized and handed over to the Spaniards. The rage of Louis XIV. and of Louvois, who had urged the opening of negotiations, taken an active part in them, and begun preparations for the occupation of Casal, may well be imagined. The Abbé d'Estrades, not less irritated, conceived a scheme of the most daring kind, proposing to Versailles nothing less than the abduction of the Mantuan minister. But Louis XIV. was determined to have no scandal. Catinat was charged with carrying out the scheme in person. The Abbé d'Estrades, in his dealings with Mattioli, feigned ignorance of the double game the Count was playing. He led him to believe, on the contrary, that the balance of the sums promised at Versailles was about to be paid. A meeting was fixed for May 2, 1679. On that day d'Estrades and Mattioli got into a carriage, the passing of which was awaited by Catinat accompanied by some dozen men. At two o'clock in the afternoon, Mattioli was in the fortress of Pignerol, in the hands of jailer Saint-Mars. When we remember the rank held by the Italian minister, we are confronted with one of the most audacious violations of international law of which history has preserved a record.

Early in the year 1694, Mattioli was transferred to the Isles of Sainte-Marguerite ; we have seen that he entered the Bastille on September 18, 1698, and died there on November 19, 1703.

The details that we possess of the imprisonment of Mattioli at Pignerol and afterwards at the Isles of Sainte-Marguerite show that he was at the outset treated with the consideration due to his rank and to the position he occupied at the time of his arrest. Eventually the respect which the prisoner had at first inspired gradually diminished : as years went on the attentions shown him grew less and less until the day when, at the Bastille, he was given a room in common with persons of the basest class. On the other hand, the rigour of his confinement, so far as the secrecy in which he was kept was concerned, was more and more relaxed ; what it was material to conceal was the circumstances under which Mattioli had been arrested, and with the lapse of time this secret continually diminished in importance. As to the mask of black velvet which Mattioli had among his possessions when he was arrested, and which he put on, without a doubt, only for the occasion, this in reality constituted a relief to his captivity, for it permitted the prisoner to leave his room, while the other state prisoners were rigorously mewed up in theirs.

It remains to prove that the masked prisoner was really Mattioli.

1. In the despatch sent by Louis XIV. to the Abbé d'Estrades five days before the arrest, the king approves the scheme of his ambassador and authorizes him to secure Mattioli, "since you believe you can get him carried off without the affair giving rise to any scandal." The prisoner is to be conducted to Pignerol, where "instructions are being sent to receive him and keep him there without anybody having knowledge of it." The

king's orders close with these words : "You must see to it that no one knows what becomes of this man." The capture effected, Catinat wrote on his part to Louvois : "It came off without any violence, and no one knows the name of the knave, not even the officers who helped to arrest him." Finally, we have a very curious pamphlet entitled *La Prudenza triomfante di Casale*, written in 1682, that is, little more than two years after the event, and—this slight detail is of capital importance —thirty years' before there was any talk of the Man in the Mask. In this we read : "The secretary (Mattioli) was surrounded by ten or twelve horsemen, who seized him, disguised him, *masked* him, and conducted him to Pignerol "—a fact, moreover, confirmed by a tradition which in the eighteenth century was still rife in the district, where scholars succeeded in culling it.

Is there any need to insist on the strength of the proofs afforded by these three documents, taken in connection one with another?

2. We know, from du Junca's register, that the masked man was shut up at Pignerol under the charge of Saint-Mars. In 1681, Saint-Mars gave up the governorship of Pignerol for that of Exiles. We can determine with absolute precision the number of prisoners Saint-Mars had then in his keeping. It was exactly five. A dispatch from Louvois, dated June 9, is very clear. In the first paragraph, he orders "the two prisoners in the lower tower" to be removed ; in the second, he adds : " The rest of the prisoners in your

charge." Here there is a clear indication of the "rest":
what follows settles the number: "The Sieur du
Chamoy has orders to pay two crowns a day for the
board of these *three* prisoners." This account, as clear
as arithmetic can make it, is further confirmed by the
letter addressed by Saint-Mars to the Abbé d'Estrades
on June 25, 1681, when he was setting out for Exiles:
"I received yesterday the warrant appointing me
governor of Exiles: I am to keep charge of two jail-
birds I have here, who have no other name than 'the
gentlemen of the lower tower'; Mattioli will remain
here with two other prisoners."

The prisoners, then, were five in number, and the
masked man is to be found, of necessity, among them.
Now we know who these five were: (1) a certain La
Rivière, who died at the end of December, 1686; (2) a
Jacobin, out of his mind, who died at the end of 1693;
(3) a certain Dubreuil, who died at the Isles of Sainte-
Marguerite about 1697. There remain Dauger and
Mattioli. The Man in the Mask is, without possible
dispute, the one or the other. We have explained above
the reasons which lead us to discard Dauger. The
mysterious prisoner, then, was Mattioli. The proof is
mathematically exact.

3. Opposite this page will be found a facsimile
reproduction of the death certificate of the masked
prisoner as inscribed on the registers of the church of
St. Paul. It is the very name of the Duke of Mantua's
former secretary that is traced there: "Marchioly." It

Burial certificate of the masked prisoner (November 20, 1703), reproduced from the facsimile in the sixth edition of *The Man in the Iron Mask*, by Marius Topin, 1883. The original, in the city archives of Paris, was destroyed in the conflagration of 1871.

must be remembered that "Marchioly" would be pronounced in Italian "Markioly," and that Saint-Mars, governor of the Bastille, who furnished the information on which the certificate was drawn up, almost always wrote in his correspondence—a characteristic detail—not "Mattioli," but "Martioly": that is the very name on the register, less distorted than the name of the major of the Bastille, who was called "Rosarges," and not "Rosage," as given on the register; and the name of the surgeon, who was called "Reilhe," and not "Reglhe."

It has been shown above how, as time went on, the rigorous seclusion to which the masked prisoner had been condemned was relaxed. What it had been thought necessary to conceal was the manner in which Mattioli had been captured, and with time that secret itself had lost its importance. As the Duke of Mantua had declared himself very well pleased with the arrest of the minister by whom he, no less than Louis XIV., had been deceived, there was nothing to prevent the name from being inscribed on a register of death, where, moreover, no one would ever have thought of looking for it.

Let us add that, in consequence of error or carelessness on the part of the officer who supplied the information for the register, or perhaps on the part of the parson or beadle who wrote it, the age is stated incorrectly, "forty-five years or thereabouts," while Mattioli was sixty-three when he died. However, the register was filled up without the least care, as a formality of no importance.

4. The Duke de Choiseul pressed Louis XV. to reveal to him the clue to the enigma. The king escaped with an evasion. One day, however, he said to him: "If you knew all about it, you would see that it has very little interest;" and some time after, when Madame de Pompadour, at de Choiseul's instigation, pressed the king on the subject, he told her that the prisoner was "the minister of an Italian prince."

In the *Memoirs of the Private Life of Marie Antoinette* by her principal lady in waiting, Madame de Campan, we read that the queen tormented Louis XVI., who did not know the secret, to have a search made among the papers of the various ministries. "I was with the queen," says Madame de Campan, "when the king, having finished his researches, told her that he had found nothing in the secret papers which had any bearing on the existence of this prisoner; that he had spoken on the subject to M. de Maurepas, whose age brought him nearer the time when the whole story must have been known to the ministers (Maurepas had been minister of the king's household as a very young man, in the early years of the eighteenth century, having the department of the *lettres de cachet*), and that M. de Maurepas had assured him that the prisoner was simply a man of a very dangerous character through his intriguing spirit, and a subject of the Duke of Mantua. He was lured to the frontier, arrested, and kept a prisoner, at first at Pignerol, then at the Bastille."

These two pieces of evidence are of such weight that

they alone would be sufficient to fix the truth. When they were written, there was no talk of Mattioli, of whose very name Madame de Campan was ignorant. Supposing that Madame de Campan had amused herself by inventing a fable—an absurd and improbable supposition, for what reason could she have had for so doing ?—it is impossible to admit that her imagination could have hit upon fancies so absolutely in accord with facts.[1]

And so the problem is solved. The legend, which had reared itself even as high as the throne of France, topples down. The satisfaction of the historian springs from his reflection that all serious historical works for more than a century, resting on far-reaching researches and eschewing all preoccupations foreign to science—such, for example, as the desire of attaining a result different from the solutions proposed by one's predecessors—have arrived at the same conclusion, which proves to be the correct solution. Heiss, Baron de Chambrier, Reth, Roux-Fazillac, Delort, Carlo Botta, Armand Baschet, Marius Topin, Paul de Saint-Victor, Camille Rousset, Chéruel, Depping, have not hesitated to place under the famous mask of black velvet the

[1] Since M. Funck-Brentano's book was published, his conclusions have been corroborated by Vicomte Maurice Boutry in a study published in the *Revue des Etudes historiques* (1899, p. 172). The Vicomte furnishes an additional proof. He says that the Duchess de Créquy, in the third book of her *Souvenirs*, gives a *résumé* of a conversation on the Iron Mask between Marshal de Noailles, the Duchess de Luynes, and others, and adds : "The most considerable and best informed persons of my time always thought that the famous story had no other foundation than the capture and captivity of the Piedmontese Mattioli."—T.

features of Mattioli. But at each new effort made by science, legend throws itself once more into the fray, gaining new activity from the passions produced by the Revolution.

The truth, in history, sometimes suggests to our mind's eye those white or yellow flowers which float on the water among broad flat leaves; a breeze springs up, a wave rises and submerges them, they disappear; but only for a moment: then they come to the surface again.

CHAPTER V.

MEN OF LETTERS IN THE BASTILLE.

SPEAKING of men of letters in France under the *ancien régime*, Michelet calls them "the martyrs of thought"; he adds: "The world thinks, France speaks. And that is precisely why the Bastille of France, the Bastille of Paris—I would rather say, the prison-house of thought —was, among all bastilles, execrable, infamous, and accursed." In the course of the article devoted to the Bastille in the *Grande Encyclopédie*, M. Fernand Bournon writes: "After Louis XIV. and throughout the eighteenth century, the Bastille was especially employed to repress, though it could not stifle, that generous and majestic movement (the glory of the human spirit) towards ideas of emancipation and enfranchisement; it was the epoch when philosophers, publicists, pamphleteers, the very booksellers, were imprisoned there in large numbers." And to substantiate this eloquent apostrophe, M. Bournon cites the names of Voltaire, La Beaumelle, the Abbé Morellet, Marmontel, and Linguet, imprisoned in the Bastille; and of Diderot and the Marquis de Mirabeau placed in the château of Vincennes.

Let us recall the story of these poor victims in turn, and trace the history of their martyrdom.

VOLTAIRE.

The most illustrious and the earliest in date of the writers mentioned by M. Bournon is Voltaire. He was sent to the Bastille on two different occasions. His first imprisonment began on May 17, 1717. At that date the poet was only twenty-two years of age and of no reputation; he did not even bear the name of Voltaire, which he only took after his discharge from the Bastille on April 14, 1718. The cause of his detention was not "the generous and majestic movement towards ideas of enfranchisement which is the glory of the human spirit," but some scurrilities which, to speak plainly, brought him what he deserved: coarse verses against the Regent and his daughter, and public utterances coarser still. Many authors state that Voltaire was imprisoned for writing the *J'ai vu*, a satire against the government of Louis XIV., each stanza of which ended with the line:—

J'ai vu ces maux, et je n'ai pas vingt ans.[1]

This is a mistake. Voltaire was imprisoned for having written the *Puero regnante*, some verses on the Regent and his daughter, the Duchess of Berry, which it would be impossible to translate. To these he added observations whose reproduction would be equally impossible. At the Bastille Voltaire underwent examinations in the usual way, in the course of which he lied with impu-

[1] "I have seen these ills, and I am not twenty yet.'

dence; after that he was allowed considerable liberty. "It was at the Bastille," wrote Condorcet, "that the young poet made the first draft of his poem *La Ligue*, corrected his tragedy of *Œdipe*, and composed some very lively lines on the ill-luck of being there."

The following are the most respectable lines of this production :—

> So one fine faultless morning in the spring,
> When Whitsun splendour brighten'd everything,
> A strange commotion startled me from sleep.
>
> . . . . .
>
> At last I reach'd my chamber in the keep.
> A clownish turnkey, with an unctuous smile,
> Of my new lodging 'gan to praise the style :
> "What ease, what charms, what comforts here are yours!
> For never Phœbus in his daily course
> Will blind you here with his too brilliant rays ;
> Within these ten-foot walls you'll spend your days
> In cool sequester'd blithefulness always."
> Then bidding me admire my cloistral cell—
> The triple doors, the triple locks as well,
> The bolts, the bars, the gratings all around—
> "'Tis but," says he, "to keep you safe and sound!"
>
> . . . . .
>
> Behold me, then, lodged in this woful place,
> Cribb'd, cabin'd, and confined in narrow space ;
> Sleepless by night, and starving half the day ;
> No joys, no friend, no mistress—wellaway![1]

When Voltaire was set at liberty, the Regent, whom, as we have just said, he had reviled, made him a very handsome offer of his protection. The poet's reply is well known : "My lord, I thank your royal highness for being so good as to continue to charge yourself with my

[1] These verses were, of course, in Latin.—T.

board, but I beseech you no longer to charge yourself with my lodging." The young writer thus obtained from the Regent a pension of 400 crowns, which later on the latter augmented to 2000 livres.

Voltaire was sent to the Bastille a second time in April, 1726. For this new detention there was no justification whatever. He had had a violent quarrel, one evening at the Opera, with the Chevalier de Rohan-Chabot. On another occasion, at the Comédie Française, the poet and the nobleman had a warm altercation in the box of Mdlle. Lecouvreur. Rohan raised his stick, Voltaire put his hand on his sword, and the actress fainted. Some days later "the gallant chevalier, assisted by half a dozen ruffians, behind whom he courageously posted himself," gave our poet a thrashing in broad daylight. When relating the adventure later, the Chevalier said pleasantly: "I commanded the squad." From that moment Voltaire sought his revenge. "The police reports reveal curious details of the loose, erratic, and feverish life he lived between the insult and his arrest," writes the careful biographer of Voltaire, Desnoiresterres. From one of these police reports we see that the young writer established relations with soldiers of the guard : several notorious bullies were constantly about him. A relative who attempted to calm him found him more irritated and violent in his language than ever. It appears certain that he was meditating some act of violence, which indeed would not have been without justification. But the Cardinal de Rohan contrived that he should be arrested on the night of April 17, 1726, and placed in the Bastille.

Speaking of this new imprisonment Marshal de Villars writes: "The public, disposed to find fault all round, came to the conclusion on this occasion that everybody was in the wrong: Voltaire for having offended the Chevalier de Rohan, the latter for having dared to commit a capital offence in causing a citizen to be beaten, the government for not having punished a notorious crime, and for having sent the injured party to the Bastille to pacify the injurer." Nevertheless, we read in the report of Hérault, the lieutenant of police: "The Sieur de Voltaire was found armed with pocket pistols, and his family, when informed of the matter, unanimously and universally applauded the wisdom of an order which saves this young man the ill effects of some new piece of folly and the worthy people who compose his family the vexation of sharing his shame."

Voltaire remained at the Bastille for *twelve days*: he was permitted to have a servant of his own choice to wait on him, who was boarded at the king's expense; as for himself, he took his meals whenever he pleased at the governor's table, going out of the Bastille, as the governor's residence stood outside the prison. Relatives and friends came to see him; his friend Thiériot dined with him; he was given pens, paper, books, whatever he desired in order to divert himself. "Using and abusing these opportunities," writes Desnoiresterres, "Voltaire believed that he could give audience to all

Paris. He wrote to those of his friends who had not yet shown a sense of their duty, exhorting them to give him proof they were alive." "I have been accustomed to all misfortunes," he wrote to Thiériot, "but not yet to that of being utterly abandoned by you. Madame de Bernières, Madame du Deffand, the Chevalier des Alleurs really ought to come and see me. They only have to ask permission of M. Hérault or M. de Maurepas." At the time of the poet's entrance to the Bastille, the lieutenant of police had written to the governor: "The Sieur de Voltaire is of a *genius* that requires humouring. His Serene Highness has approved of my writing to tell you that the king's intention is that you should secure for him mild treatment and the internal liberty of the Bastille, so far as these do not jeopardize the security of his detention." The warrant setting him at liberty was signed on April 26.

La Beaumelle.

In M. Bournon's list La Beaumelle comes second. The circumstances under which he was put into the Bastille were as follows. After having fallen out at Berlin with Voltaire, whom he had compared to a monkey, La Beaumelle returned to Paris, whence he had been exiled. There he got printed a new edition of Voltaire's *Age of Louis XIV.*, unknown to the author, and interpolated therein odes insulting to the house of Orleans. "La Beaumelle," exclaimed Voltaire, "is the first who dared to print another man's work in his lifetime. This miserable

Erostrates of the *Age of Louis XIV.* has discovered the secret of changing into an infamous libel, for fifteen ducats, a work undertaken for the glory of the nation."

La Beaumelle became an inmate of the Bastille in April, 1753, and remained there for six months. Writing on May 18, 1753, to M. Roques, Voltaire said that "there was scarcely any country where he would not inevitably have been punished sooner or later, and I know from a certain source that there are two courts where they would have inflicted a chastisement more signal than that which he is undergoing here."

It was not long before La Beaumelle issued his edition of *Notes towards the History of Madame de Maintenon and that of the past century*, with nine volumes of correspondence. He had fabricated letters which he attributed to Madame de Saint-Géran and Madame de Frontenac, and published a correspondence of Madame de Maintenon which M. Geffroy, in a work recognized as authoritative, regards as full of barefaced falsehoods and foul and scurrilous inventions. He had inserted in his work the following phrase: "The court of Vienna has been long accused of having poisoners always in its pay."

It must be observed that La Beaumelle's publication owed its great vogue to special circumstances. The author's reputation abroad, the very title of the book, lent it great importance; and France, then engaged in the Seven Years' War, found it necessary to keep in Austria's good graces. La Beaumelle was conveyed to the Bastille a second time. The lieutenant of police, Berryer, put him through the usual examination. La Beaumelle was a man of the world, so witty that in the course of their quarrels he drove Voltaire himself to despair. He showed himself such in his examination. "La Beaumelle," said Berryer to him, "this is wit you are giving me when what I ask of you is plain sense." On his expressing a wish for a companion, he was placed with the Abbé d'Estrades. The officers of the château had all his manuscripts brought from his house, so that he might continue his literary work. He had at the Bastille a library of 600 volumes, ranged on shelves which the governor ordered to be made for him. He there finished a translation of the *Annals* of Tacitus and the *Odes* of Horace. He had permission to write to his relatives and friends, and to receive visits from them; he had the liberty of walking in the castle garden, of breeding birds in his room, and of having brought from outside all the luxuries to which he was partial. The principal secretary of the lieutenant of police, Duval, reports the following incident: "Danry (the famous Latude) and Allègre (his companion in confinement and ere long in escape) found means to open a correspondence with all the prisoners in the Bastille. They lifted a stone in a closet of the chapel, and put their letters underneath it. La Beaumelle pretended to be a woman in his letters to Allègre, and as he was a man of parts and Allègre was of keen sensibility and an excellent writer, the latter fell madly in love with La Beaumelle, to such a degree that, though they mutually agreed to burn their letters, Allègre preserved those of his fancied mistress, which he had not the heart to give to the flames ; with the result that, the letters being discovered at an inspection of his room, he was put in the cells for some time. The prisoner amused himself also by composing verses which he recited at the top of his voice. This gave much concern to the officers of the garrison, and Chevalier, the major, wrote to the lieutenant of police on the matter: "The Sieur de la Beaumelle seems to have gone clean out of his mind; he seems to be a maniac ; he amuses himself by declaiming verses in his room for a part of the day : for the rest of the time he is quiet."

This second detention lasted from August, 1756, till August, 1757.

The Abbé Morellet.

We come to the Abbé Morellet, a man of fine and fascinating mind, one of the best of the Encyclopædists, who died in 1819 a member of the Institute and the object of general esteem. He was arrested on June 11, 1760, for having had printed and distributed, without privilege or permission, a pamphlet entitled : *Preface to the Philosophers' Comedy ; or, the Vision of Charles Palissot.*[1] These are the terms in which, later on, Morellet himself judged his pamphlet : "I must here make my confession.

[1] Palissot was a dramatist and critic who in his comedy *Les Philosophes* had bitterly attacked Rousseau, Diderot, and the Encyclopædists generally.—T.

In this work, I went far beyond the limits of a literary pleasantry regarding the Sieur Palissot, and to-day I am not without remorse for my fault." And further, as J. J. Rousseau, in whose favour the pamphlet had been in part composed, had to acknowledge, the Abbé "very impudently" insulted a young and pretty woman, Madame de Robecq, who was dying of decline, spitting blood, and did actually die a few days later.

The arrest of Morellet was demanded by Malesherbes, then censor of the press, one of the most generous and liberal spirits of the time, the inspirer of the famous remonstrances of the Court of Taxation against *lettres de cachet*—the man who, as M. H. Monin testifies, "being elected censor of the press, protected philosophers and men of letters, and by his personal efforts facilitated the publication of the *Encyclopædia*." Speaking of the *Preface to the Comedy*, Malesherbes writes to Gabriel de Sartine, lieutenant-general of police: "It is an outrageous pamphlet, not only against Palissot, but against respectable persons whose very condition should shelter them against such insults. I beg you, sir, to be good enough to put a stop to this scandal. I believe it to be a matter of public importance that the punishment should be very severe, and that this punishment should not stop at the Bastille or the For-l'Evêque,[1] because a very wide distinction must be drawn between the delinquencies

---

[1] The old prison of Paris. It was the debtors' prison, famous also for the number of actors who were imprisoned there under the *ancien régime*. It was demolished in 1780.—T.

of men of letters tearing each other to pieces and the insolence of those who attack persons of the highest consideration in the State. I do not think that Bicêtre would be too severe for these last. If you have to ask M. de Saint-Florentin for the royal authority for your proceedings, I hope you will be good enough to inform him of the request I am making."

It will be observed that, on Malesherbes' showing, the Bastille would not suffice to punish the *Preface to the Comedy*, nor even the For-l'Evêque; he asks for the most stringent of the prisons, Bicêtre. Before long, it is true, this excellent man returned to milder sentiments. An imprisonment at Bicêtre, he wrote, would be infamous. Saint-Florentin and Sartine were not hard to convince. Morellet was taken to the Bastille. " The warrant for his arrest," wrote one of his agents to Malesherbes, "was executed this morning by Inspector D'Hémery with all the amenities possible in so unpleasant a business. D'Hémery knows the Abbé Morellet, and has spoken of him to M. de Sartine in the most favourable terms."

When he entered the Bastille the Abbé calculated that his imprisonment would last six months, and after acknowledging that he at that time viewed his detention without great distress, he adds : "I am bound to say, to lower the too high opinion that may be formed of me and my courage, that I was marvellously sustained by a thought which rendered my little virtue more easy. I saw some literary glory illumining the walls of my prison ; persecuted, I must be better known. The men of letters whom I had avenged, and the philosophy for which I was a martyr, would lay the foundation of my reputation. The men of the world, who love satire, would receive me better than ever. A career was opening before me, and I should be able to pursue it at greater advantage. These six months at the Bastille would be an excellent recommendation, and would infallibly make my fortune."

The Abbé remained at the Bastille, not six months, but six weeks, "which slipped away," he observes "—I chuckle still as I think of them—very pleasantly for me." He spent his time in reading romances, and, with admirable humour, in writing a *Treatise on the Liberty of the Press*. Afterwards the good Abbé informs us that the hopes which he had indulged were not deceived. On issuing from the Bastille he was a made man. Little known two months before, he now met everywhere with the reception he desired. The doors of the salons of Madame de Boufflers, Madame Necker, the Baron d'Holbach, flew open before him; women pitied him and admired him, and men followed their example. Why have we not to-day a Bastille to facilitate the career of writers of talent !

Marmontel.

To Marmontel his stay at the royal prison appeared as pleasant as the Abbé Morellet had found his. He had amused himself by reciting at Madame Geoffrin's a mordant satire in which the Duke d'Aumont, first groom of the stole to the king, was cruelly hit. The duke expostulated; Marmontel wrote to him declaring that he was not the author of the satire; but the nobleman stood his ground.

"I am helpless," said the Count de Saint-Florentin, who countersigned the *lettre de cachet*, to Marmontel; "the Duke d'Aumont accuses you, and is determined to have you punished. It is a satisfaction he demands in recompense for his services and the services of his ancestors. The king has been pleased to grant him his wish. So you will go and find M. de Sartine; I am addressing to him the king's order; you will tell him that it was from my hand you received it."

"I went to find M. de Sartine," writes Marmontel, "and I found with him the police officer who was to accompany me. M. de Sartine was intending that he should go to the Bastille in a separate carriage; but I myself declined this obliging offer, and we arrived at the Bastille, my introducer and myself, in the same hack. . . . The governor, M. d'Abadie, asked me if I wished my servant to be left with me. . . . They made a cursory inspection of my packets and books, and then sent me up to a large room furnished with two beds, two tables, a low cupboard, and three cane chairs. It was cold, but a jailer made us a good fire and brought me wood in abundance. At the same time they gave me pens, ink, and paper, on condition of my accounting for the use I made of them and the number of sheets they allowed me.

"The jailer came back to ask if I was satisfied with

my bed. After examining it I replied that the mattresses were bad and the coverlets dirty. In a minute all was changed. They sent to ask me what was my dinner hour. I replied, 'The same as everybody's.' The Bastille had a library: the governor sent me the catalogue, giving me free choice among the books. I merely thanked him for myself, but my servant asked for the romances of Prévost, and they were brought to him."

Let us go on with Marmontel's story. "For my part," he says, "I had the means of escape from ennui. Having been for a long time impatient of the contempt shown by men of letters for Lucan's poem, which they had not read, and only knew in the barbarous fustian of Brébeuf's version, I had resolved to translate it more becomingly and faithfully into prose; and this work, which would occupy me without fatiguing my brain, was the best possible employment for the solitary leisure of my prison. So I had brought the *Pharsalia* with me, and, to understand it the better, I had been careful to bring with it the *Commentaries* of Cæsar. Behold me then at the corner of a good fire, pondering the quarrel of Cæsar and Pompey, and forgetting my own with the Duke d'Aumont. And there was Bury too (Marmontel's servant) as philosophical as myself, amusing himself by making our beds placed at two opposite corners of my room, which was at this moment lit up by the beams of a fine winter sun, in spite of the bars of two strong iron gratings which permitted me a view of the Suburb Saint-Antoine.

"Two hours later, the noise of the bolts of the two doors which shut me in startled me from my profound musings, and the two jailers, loaded with a dinner I believed to be mine, came in and served it in silence. One put down in front of the fire three little dishes covered with plates of common earthenware; the other laid on that one of the two tables which was clear a tablecloth rather coarse, indeed, but white. I saw him place on the table a very fair set of things, a pewter spoon and fork, good household bread, and a bottle of wine. Their duty done, the jailers retired, and the two doors were shut again with the same noise of locks and bolts.

"Then Bury invited me to take my place, and served my soup. It was a Friday. The soup, made without meat, was a *purée* of white beans, with the freshest butter, and a dish of the same beans was the first that Bury served me with. I found all this excellent. The dish of cod he gave me for second course was better still. It was served with a dash of garlic, which gave it a delicacy of taste and odour which would have flattered the taste of the daintiest Gascon. The wine was not first-rate, but passable; no sweets: of course one must expect to be deprived of something. On the whole, I thought that dinner in prison was not half bad.

"As I was rising from table, and Bury was about to sit down—for there was enough for his dinner in what was left—lo and behold! in came my two jailers again, with pyramids of dishes in their hands. At this display of fine linen, fine china-ware, spoon and fork of silver, we recognized our mistake; but we made not the ghost of a sign, and when our jailers, having laid down their burden, had retired, 'Sir,' said Bury, 'you have just eaten my dinner, you will quite agree to my having my turn and eating yours.' 'That's fair,' I replied, and the walls of my room were astonished, I fancy, at the sound of laughter.

"This dinner was not vegetarian; here are the details: an excellent soup, a juicy beef-steak, a boiled capon's leg streaming with gravy and melting in one's mouth, a little dish of artichokes fried in pickle, a dish of spinach, a very fine William pear, fresh-cut grapes, a bottle of old burgundy, and best Mocha coffee; this was Bury's dinner, with the exception of the coffee and the fruit, which he insisted on reserving for me.

"After dinner the governor came to see me, and asked me if I found the fare sufficient, assuring me that I should be served from his table, that he would take care to cut my portions himself, and that no one should touch my food but himself. He suggested a fowl for my supper; I thanked him and told him that what was left of the fruit from my dinner would suffice. The reader has just seen what my ordinary fare was at the Bastille, and from this he may infer with what mildness, or rather reluctance, they brought themselves to visit on me the wrath of the Duke d'Aumont.

"Every day I had a visit from the governor. As he had some smack of literature and even of Latin, he took some interest in following my work, in fact, enjoyed it; but soon, tearing himself away from these little dissipations, he said, 'Adieu, I am going to console men who are more unfortunate than you.'"

Such was the imprisonment of Marmontel. It lasted for eleven days.

LINGUET.

Linguet, advocate and journalist, was arrested for a breach of the press laws and for slander. He was a man of considerable ability, but little character. Attorney-general Cruppi has devoted to the story of Linguet a work as extensive as it is eloquent. He has a wealth of indulgence for his hero; yet, despite the goodwill he shows for him and endeavours to impart to the reader, his book reveals between the lines that Linguet was worthy of little esteem, and that his professional brethren were justified in removing his name from the roll of the advocates of Paris.

Linguet's captivity lasted for two years. He has left a description of it in his *Memoirs on the Bastille*, which made a great noise, and of which the success has endured down to our own day. His book, like everything which came from his pen, is written in a fluent style, with spirit and brilliance; the facts cited are for the most part correct, but the author, aiming at making a sensation, has cleverly presented them in a light which distorts their real character. "There are means," says Madame de Staal, "of so distributing light and shade on the facts one is exhibiting, as to alter their appearance without altering the groundwork." Take, for instance, the description that Linguet gives of his belongings while in the Bastille: "Two worm-eaten mattresses, a cane chair the seat of which was only held to it by strings, a folding table, a jug for water, two earthenware pots, one of them for drinking, and two stone slabs to make a fire on." A contemporary could say of Linguet's *Memoirs*, "It is the longest lie that ever was printed." And yet, if we take the facts themselves which are related by the clever journalist, and disengage them from the deceitful mirage in which he has enwrapped them, we do not see that his life in the Bastille was so wretched as he endeavours to make us believe. He is forced to acknowledge that his food was always most abundant, adding, it is true, that that was because they wished to poison him! He owed his life, he is convinced, "only to the obstinate tenacity of his constitution." He marked, nevertheless, on the *menu* for the day, which was sent up every morning by the Bastille cook, the dishes he fancied; and later on he had his room furnished after his own heart. He still enjoyed, moreover, enough liberty to write during his imprisonment a work entitled, *The Trials of Three Kings, Louis XVI., Charles III., and George III.*, which appeared in London in 1781. Let us recall once more the famous saying of Linguet to the wig-maker of the Bastille on the first day that he presented himself to trim the prisoner's beard: "To whom have I the honour of speaking?" "I am, sir, the barber to the Bastille." "Gad, then, why don't you raze it?"

In June, 1792, some years after his liberation, Linguet was prosecuted a second time for breach of the press laws. The revolutionary tribunal condemned him to death. As he mounted the steps of the scaffold, the ardent pamphleteer thought, mayhap, with bitterly ironical regret, of that Bastille whose destruction he had so clamorously demanded.

DIDEROT.

We have still to speak of Diderot and the Marquis de Mirabeau, who were not incarcerated at the Bastille, but at Vincennes, not in the castle keep, but in the château itself, which constituted a separate place of imprisonment. They placed in the château only prisoners guilty of minor offences, who were sentenced to a temporary detention, and to whom they wished to show some consideration. This was, as we have just said, the abode of Diderot and the Marquis de Mirabeau. Diderot was arrested on July 24, 1749. His last book, *Letters on the Blind for the Use of those Who Can See*, contained theories which appeared to have but little title to the description of "moral." But in the course of his examination he stoutly denied that he was its author, as also he denied the authorship of the *Thoughts of a Philosopher* he had published some years before. The lieutenant of police gave instructions to the governor of Vincennes that, short of being set at liberty, Diderot was to be granted all possible comforts—allowed to walk in the garden and park; "that the king's desire was, in consideration of the literary work on which he was engaged (the *Encyclopædia*), to permit him to communicate freely with persons from without who might come for that purpose or on family business." And so Diderot received a visit from his wife and walked with her in the wood; Rousseau and D'Alembert spent their afternoons with him, and, as in the "good old days" of Plato and Socrates, our philosophers chatted of metaphysics and love, seated on the green grass under the shade of mighty oaks. The booksellers and printers who had undertaken the publication of the *Encyclopædia* were, as we have seen, in constant communication with Diderot at Vincennes; he corrected in prison the proofs of the publication, which the court looked on with no favourable eye. And we know, too, that at night, with the secret complicity of the governor, our philosopher cleared the park walls to hurry to a fair lady at Paris, one Madame de Puysieux, whom he loved with a passion by no means platonic; ere the sun was up, the jailers found him safely back under lock and key. This irksome captivity lasted little more than three months.

THE MARQUIS DE MIRABEAU.

The imprisonment of Mirabeau lasted only ten days. The *lettre de cachet* had been obtained by the clique of financiers, who took fright at the audacious conceptions of the *Theory of Taxation*. "I fancy I deserved my punishment," wrote the Marquis, "like the ass in the fable, for a clumsy and misplaced zeal." In regard to the arrest, Madame d'Epinay sent word to Voltaire : "Never before was a man arrested as this one was. The officer said to him, 'Sir, my orders do not state I am to hurry you : to-morrow will do, if you haven't time to-day.' 'No, sir, one cannot be too prompt in obeying the king's orders, I am quite ready.' And off he went with a bag crammed with books and papers." At Vincennes the Marquis had a servant with him. His wife came to see him. The king spent for his support fifteen livres a day, more than twenty-five shillings of our money. He was liberated on December 24, 1760. His brother, Bailie Mirabeau, speaking of this detention, wrote to him of "a week's imprisonment in which you were shown every possible consideration."

We have exhausted M. Bournon's list of the writers who were victims of arbitrary authority. Such are the "martyrs" for whom that excellent historian, and Michelet and others, have shown the most affecting compassion. The foregoing facts do not call for comment. Men of letters were the spoilt children of the eighteenth century much more than of our own, and never has an absolute government shown a toleration equal to that of the monarchy under the *ancien régime* towards writers whose doctrines, as events have proved, tended directly to its destruction.

CHAPTER VI.

LATUDE.

FEW historical figures have taken a higher place in the popular imagination than Masers de Latude. That celebrated prisoner seems to have accumulated in his life of suffering all the wrongs that spring from an arbitrary government. The novelists and playwrights of the nineteenth century have made him a hero; the poets have draped his woes in fine mourning robes, our greatest historians have burnt for him the midnight oil; numerous editions of his *Memoirs* have appeared in quick succession down to our own days. Even by his contemporaries he was regarded as a martyr, and posterity has not plucked the shining crown of martyrdom from his head, hoary with the snows of long captivity. His legend is the creature of his own unaided brain. When in 1790 he dictated the story of his life, he made greater calls on his glowing southern imagination than on his memory; but the documents relating to his case in the archives of the Bastille have been preserved. At the present time they are to be found dispersed among various libraries, at the Arsenal, at Carnavalet, at St.

Petersburg. Thanks to them it is easy to establish the truth.

On March 23, 1725, at Montagnac in Languedoc, a poor girl named Jeanneton Aubrespy gave birth to a male child who was baptized three days later under the name of Jean Henri, given him by his god-parents, Jean Bouhour and Jeanne Boudet. Surname the poor little creature had none, for he was the illegitimate child of a father unknown. Jeanneton, who had just passed her thirtieth year, was of respectable middle-class family, and lived near the Lom gate in a little house which seems to have been her own. Several cousins of hers held commissions in the army. But from the day when she became a mother, her family had no more to do with her, and she fell into want. Happily she was a woman of stout heart, and by her spinning and sewing she supported her boy, who shot up into a lad of keen intelligence and considerable ambition. She succeeded in getting him some sort of education, and we find Jean Henri at the age of seventeen acting as assistant surgeon in the army of Languedoc. Surgeons, it is true, made no great figure in the eighteenth century; they combined the duties of barber and dentist as well as leech. But the situation was good enough. "Assistant surgeons in the army," wrote Saint-Marc the detective, "who really worked at their trade, made a good deal of money." At this time, being reluctant to bear his mother's name, the young man ingeniously transformed his double forename into Jean Danry, under which he is designated in a passport for Alsace, given him on March 25, 1743, by the general commanding the royal forces in Languedoc. In the same year 1743, Danry accompanied the army of Marshal de Noailles in its operations on the Maine and the Rhine, receiving from the Marshal, towards the end of the season, a certificate testifying to his good and faithful service throughout the campaign.

Four years later we find Danry at Brussels, employed in the field-hospital of the army in Flanders, at a salary of 500 livres a month. He was present at the famous siege of Bergen-op-Zoom, the impregnable fortress which the French so valiantly stormed under the command of the Comte de Lowendal. But peace being concluded at Aix-la-Chapelle, the armies were disbanded, and Danry went to Paris. He had in his pocket a letter of recommendation to Descluzeaux, the surgeon of Marshal de Noailles, and a certificate signed by Guignard de La Garde, chief of the commissariat, testifying to the ability and good conduct of "the aforesaid Jean Danry, assistant surgeon." These two certificates formed the most substantial part of his fortune.

Danry arrived in Paris about the end of the year 1748. On any afternoon he might have been seen strolling about the Tuileries in a grey frock and red waistcoat, carrying his twenty-three years with a good grace. Of middle height and somewhat spare figure, wearing his brown hair in a silk net, having keen eyes and an expression of much intelligence, he would probably have been thought a handsome fellow but for the marks which smallpox had indelibly stamped on his face. His accent had a decided Gascon tang, and it is obvious, from the spelling of his letters, not only that he could not boast of a literary education, but that his speech was that of a man of the people. Yet, what with his brisk temperament, his professional skill, and his favour with his superiors, he was in a fair way to attain an honourable position, which would have enabled him at length to support his mother, then living in solitary friendlessness at Montagnac, centring on him, in her forlorn condition, all her affection and her dearest hopes.

Paris, with its gaiety and stir, dazzled the young man. Its brilliant and luxurious life, its rustling silks and laces, set him dreaming. He found the girls of Paris charming creatures, and opened his heart to them without stint, and his purse too; and his heart was more opulent than his purse. Ere long he had spent his modest savings and sunk into want. He fell into bad company. His best friend, an apothecary's assistant named Binguet, shared with him a mean garret in the Cul-de-sac du Coq, in the house of one Charmeleux, who let furnished lodgings. Than these two no greater rakes, wastrels, or thorough-paced rascals could have been found in all Paris. Danry in particular very soon got a name all over his neighbourhood for his riotous, threatening, and choleric temper. Dying of hunger, threatened with being ejected neck-and-crop from his lodging for non-payment of rent, he was reduced at last to write for money to his mother, who, poor thing, had barely enough for her own modest wants.

As yet we are a long way from the "handsome officer of engineers" who lives in our remembrance: we see little likeness to the brilliant picture which Danry drew later of those youthful years during which he received, "by the care of his father the Marquis de La Tude, the education of a gentleman destined to serve his country and his king."

Having come now absolutely to the end of his resources, Danry took it into his head that, at the siege of Bergen-op-Zoom, he had been stripped by some soldiers of all his clothes but his shirt, and robbed of 678 livres into the bargain. This story he worked up in a letter addressed to Moreau de Séchelles, commissary of the army in Flanders, hoping to get it corroborated by Guignard de La Garde, the commissary under whom he had himself served. In this letter he demanded compensation for the losses he had suffered while devoting himself under fire to the care of the wounded. But we read, in the *Memoirs* he wrote later, that so far from having been stripped and robbed, he had actually purchased at Bergen-op-Zoom a considerable quantity of goods of all kinds when they were sold off cheap after the sack of the town. However that may be, his experiment was a failure. But Danry was a man of resource, and not many days had passed before he had hit on another means of raising the wind.

At this time everybody was talking about the struggle

Cover of the explosive box sent by Danry to the Marquise de Pompadour. The words almost obliterated are: "Je vous prie, Madame, d'ouvrir le paquet en particulié." Below is the record and the date of Danry's examination, with his signature, and that of Berryer, the lieutenant of police.

between the king's ministers and the Marquise de Pompadour, which had just ended in a triumph for the lady. Maurepas was going into exile, but it was generally believed that he was a man who would wreak vengeance on his enemy, and the favourite herself openly declared that she went in fear of poison. A light dawned on the young surgeon's mind as he heard such gossip as this; he caught a sudden glimpse of himself—even he, the ragged outcast—arrayed in cloth of gold and rolling in his carriage along the Versailles road.

This was his plan. On April 27, 1749, in a shop under the arcade of the Palais-Royal, hard by the grand staircase, he bought of a small tradesman six of those little bottle-shaped toys, once called Prince Rupert's Drops, out of which children used to get so much harmless amusement. They were globules of molten glass, which, on being thrown into cold water, had taken the shape of pears, and which, if the tapering end was suddenly snapped, crumbled with a loud report into dust. Four of these crackers Danry placed in a cardboard box, binding the thin ends together with a thread which he fixed in the lid. Over these he sprinkled some toilet powder, and this he covered with a layer of powdered vitriol and alum. The whole packet he then enclosed in a double wrapper, writing on the inner one, "I beg you, madam, to open the packet in private," and on the outer one, "To Madame the Marquise de Pompadour, at court."

At eight o'clock in the evening of the next day,

Danry, having seen his packet safely in the post, hurried off himself to Versailles. He had hoped to gain admittance to the favourite herself, but being stopped by Gourbillon, her principal valet, in a voice trembling with emotion he related to him a frightful story. Happening to be at the Tuileries, he said, he had observed two men seated in animated conversation, and on going close to them heard them mouthing the most horrible threats against Madame de Pompadour. When they rose he dogged their footsteps, which led direct to the post office, where they consigned a packet to the box. Who the men were, and what was the nature of the packet, were natural questions to which Danry had no answer: all he could say was that, devoted to the interests of the Marquise, he had instantly sped off to reveal to her what he had seen.

To understand the impression produced by the young man's information, it is necessary to bear in mind the feverish excitement then prevailing at court. Maurepas, the witty and sprightly minister who had won Louis XV.'s special affection because of the charm with which he endowed mere business for "the man who was always bored"—Maurepas had just been exiled to Bourges. "Pontchartrain," the king sent word to him, "is too near." The struggle between the minister and the favourite had been one of extraordinary violence. Maurepas was for ever dashing off satirical verses on the girl who had reached the steps of the throne, and incessantly pursuing her with the cruel and insolent shafts of his wit ; his muse indeed did not shrink from the most brutal insults. Nor was the Marquise a whit more tender towards her foe: she openly dubbed him liar and knave, and assured everybody that he was trying to get her poisoned. A surgeon was actually required to be in constant attendance upon her, and she always had an antidote within reach. At table she was careful never to be the first to partake of any dish, and in her box at the theatre she would drink no lemonade but what had been prepared by her surgeon.

The packet which Danry had posted arrived at Versailles on April 29, and Quesnay, the physician to the king and the Marquise, was requested to open it. Having done so with infinite precaution, he recognized the vitriol and alum and toilet powder, and declared at once that there was not a pennyworth of danger in the whole contrivance. But since alum and vitriol were substances capable of being turned to baneful uses, he thought that possibly it was a case of a criminal design clumsily executed.

There is not a shadow of doubt that Louis XV. and his mistress were seriously alarmed. D'Argenson himself, who had upheld Maurepas against the favourite, had the greatest possible interest in seeing the affair cleared up as soon as possible. The first move was altogether in favour of the informer. D'Argenson wrote to Berryer that Danry was deserving of a reward.

No time was lost in instituting a search for the authors

of the plot. The lieutenant of police selected the most skilful and intelligent of his officers, the detective Saint-Marc, who put himself in communication with Danry. But he had not spent two days with the assistant surgeon before he drew up a report demanding his arrest. "It is not unimportant to note that Danry is a surgeon, and his best friend an apothecary. In my opinion it is essential to apprehend both Danry and Binguet without further delay, and without letting either know of the other's arrest, and at the same time to search their rooms."

Accordingly Danry was conveyed to the Bastille on May 1, 1749, and Binguet was secured the same day. Saint-Marc had taken the precaution to ask the assistant surgeon for a written account of his adventure. This document he put into the hands of an expert, who compared the handwriting with the address on the packet sent to Versailles. Danry was lost. Suspicion was but too well confirmed by the results of a search in his room. Being shut up in the Bastille, Danry knew nothing of all these proceedings, and when, on May 2, the lieutenant-general of police came to question him, he replied only with lies.

Berryer, the lieutenant of police, was a man of much firmness, but honourable and kindly disposed. "He inspired one's confidence," wrote Danry himself, "by his urbanity and kindness." This excellent man was vexed at the attitude taken up by the prisoner, and pointing out the danger he was incurring, he besought him to tell the truth. But at a second examination Danry only persisted in his lies. Then all at once he changed his tactics and refused to answer the questions put to him. "Danry, here we do justice to every one," said Berryer to him, to give him courage. But entreaties had no better success than threats. Danry maintained his obstinate silence; and D'Argenson wrote to Berryer: "The thorough elucidation of this affair is too important for you not to follow up any clue which may point towards a solution."

By his falsehoods, and then by his silence, Danry had succeeded in giving the appearance of a mysterious plot to what was really an insignificant piece of knavery.

Not till June 15 did he make up his mind to offer a statement very near the truth, which was written down and sent at once to the king, who read it over several times and kept it in his pocket the whole day—a circumstance which indicates to what importance the affair had now swelled. Suspicions were not dispelled by the declaration of June 15. Danry had misrepresented the truth in his former examinations, and there was reason to believe that he was equally misrepresenting it in the third. Thus he owed his ruin to his silence and his self-contradictory depositions. Six months later, on October 7, 1749, when he was at Vincennes, Dr. Quesnay, who had shown much interest in the young surgeon, was sent to find out from him the name of the individual who had instigated the crime. On his return the doctor wrote to Berryer, "My journey has been utterly useless. I only saw a blockhead, who persisted nevertheless in adhering to his former declarations." Two years more had passed away when the lieutenant of police wrote to Quesnay:—"February 25, 1751. Danry would be very glad if you would pay him a visit, and your compliance might perhaps induce him to lay bare his secret soul, and make a frank confession to you of what up to the present he has obstinately concealed from me."

Quesnay at once repaired to the Bastille, bearing with him a conditional promise of liberty. Working himself up into a frenzy, Danry swore that "all his answers to the lieutenant of police had been strictly true." When the doctor had taken his leave, Danry wrote to the minister: "M. Quesnay, who has been several times to see me in my wretchedness, tells me that your lordship is inclined to believe I had some accomplice in my fault whom I will not reveal, and that it is for this reason your lordship will not give me my liberty. I could wish, my lord, from the bottom of my heart, that your belief were true, for it would be much to my profit to put my guilt upon another, whether for having induced me to commit my sin or for not having prevented me from committing it."

It was the opinion of the ministers that Danry had been the instrument of a plot against the life of the Marquise de Pompadour directed by some person of high rank, and that at the critical moment he had either taken fright, or else had made a clean breast of the matter at Versailles in the hope of reaping some advantage from both sides. These facts must be kept in mind if we are to understand the real cause of his confinement. Kept, then, in the Bastille, he was subjected to several examinations, the reports of which were regularly drawn up and signed by the lieutenant of police. Under the *ancien régime*, this officer was, as we have seen, a regular magistrate, indeed he has no other designation in the documents of the period; he pronounced sentence and awarded punishments in accordance with that body of customs which then, as to-day in England, constituted the law.

Binguet, the apothecary, had been set at liberty immediately after Danry's declaration of June 15. In the Bastille, Danry was treated with the utmost consideration, in accordance with the formal instructions of Berryer. He was provided with books, tobacco, and a pipe; he was permitted to play on the flute; and having declared that a solitary life bored him, he was given two room mates. Every day he was visited by the officers of the fortress, and on May 25 the governor came to tell him of the magistrate's order: "That the utmost attention was to be shown him; if he needed anything he was to be requested to say so, and was to be allowed to want for nothing." No doubt the lieutenant of police hoped, by dint of kindness, to persuade him to disclose the authors of the unfortunate plot which was the figment of his imagination.

Danry did not remain long in the prison of the Suburb Saint-Antoine; on July 28 Saint-Marc transferred him to Vincennes, and we see from the report drawn up by the detective with what astonishment the Marquis du Châtelet, governor of the fortress, heard "that the court had resolved to send him such a fellow." Vincennes, like the Bastille, was reserved for prisoners of good position; our hero was sent there by special favour, as he was told for his consolation by the surgeon who attended him: "Only persons of noble birth or the highest distinction are sent to Vincennes." Danry was indeed treated like a lord. The best apartment was reserved for him, and he was able to enjoy the park, where he walked for two hours every day. At the time of his admission to the Bastille, he was suffering from some sort of indisposition which later on he ascribed to his long confinement. At Vincennes he complained of the same illness, with the same plea that his troubles had made him ill. He was attended by a specialist as well as by the surgeon of the prison.

Meantime the lieutenant came again to see him, reiterating assurances of his protection, and advising him to write direct to Madame de Pompadour. Here is what Danry wrote:—

"VINCENNES, *November* 4, 1749.

"MADAM,—If wretchedness, goaded by famine, has driven me to commit a fault against your dear person, it was with no design of doing you any mischief. God is my witness. If the divine mercy would assure you to-day, on my behalf, how my soul repents of its heinous fault, and how for 188 days I have done nothing but weep at the sight of my iron bars, you would have pity on me. Madam, for the sake of God who is enlightening you, let your just wrath soften at the spectacle of my repentance, my wretchedness, my tears. One day God will recompense you for your humanity. You are all-powerful, Madam; God has given you power with the greatest king on all the earth, His well-beloved; he is merciful, he is not cruel, he is a Christian. If the divine power moves your magnanimity to grant me my freedom, I would rather die, or sustain my life on nothing but roots, than jeopardize it a second time. I have staked all my hopes on your Christian charity. Lend a sympathetic ear to my prayer, do not abandon me to my unhappy fate. I hope in you, Madam, and God will vouchsafe an abundant answer to my prayers that your dear person may obtain your heart's desires.

"I have the honour to be, with a repentance worthy of pardon, Madam, your very humble and very obedient servant,   "DANRY."

A letter which it is a pleasure to quote, for it snows to great advantage beside the letters written later by the prisoner. It was only the truth that he had no evil design on the favourite's life; but soon becoming more audacious, he wrote to Madame de Pompadour saying that if he had addressed the box to her at

Versailles, it was out of pure devotion to her, to put her on her guard against the machinations of her enemies, in short, to save her life.

Danry's letter was duly forwarded to the Marquise, but remained without effect. Losing patience, he resolved to win for himself the freedom denied him: on June 15, 1750, he escaped.

In his *Memoirs* Danry has related the story of this first escape in a manner as lively as imaginative. He really eluded his jailers in the simplest way in the world. Having descended to the garden at the usual hour for his walk, he found there a black spaniel frisking about. The dog happened to rear itself against the gate, and to push it with its paws. The gate fell open. Danry passed out and ran straight ahead, " till, towards four o'clock in the afternoon, he fell to the ground with fatigue, in the neighbourhood of Saint-Denis."

There he remained until nine o'clock in the evening. Then he struck into the road to Paris, passing the night beside the aqueduct near the Saint-Denis gate. At daybreak he entered the city.

We know what importance was attached at court to the safe custody of the prisoner: there was still hope that he would make up his mind to speak of the grave conspiracy of which he held the secret. D'Argenson wrote at once to Berryer: "Nothing is more important or more urgent than to set on foot at once all conceivable means of recapturing the prisoner." Accordingly all the police were engaged in the search; the description of the prisoner was printed, a large number of copies being distributed by Inspector Rulhière among the mounted police.

Danry took up his lodging with one Cocardon, at the sign of the Golden Sun; but he did not venture to remain for more than two days in the same inn. He expected his old chum Binguet to come to his assistance, but Binguet was not going to have anything more to do with the Bastille. It was a pretty girl, Annette Benoist, whom Danry had known when he was lodging with Charmeleux, that devoted herself heart and soul to him. She knew she herself was running the risk of imprisonment, and already strangers of forbidding appearance had come asking at the Golden Sun who she was. Little she cared; she found assistance among her companions: the girls carried Danry's letters and undertook the search for a safe lodging. Meanwhile, Danry went to pass the night under the aqueducts; in the morning he shut himself in the lodging the girls had chosen for him, and there he remained for two days without leaving the house, Annette coming there to keep him company. Unluckily the young man had no money: how was he to pay his score? "What was to be done, what was to become of me?" he said later. "I was sure to be discovered if I showed myself; if I fled I ran no less risk." He wrote to Dr. Quesnay, who had shown him so much kindness at Vincennes; but the police got wind of the letter, and Saint-Marc arrived and seized the fugitive in the inn where he lay concealed. The unlucky wretch was haled back to the Bastille. Annette was arrested at the Golden Sun at the moment when she was asking for Danry's letters; she too was shut up in the Bastille. The warders and sentinels who were on duty at Vincennes on the day of the escape had been thrown into the cells.

By his escape from Vincennes, Danry had doubled the gravity of his offence. The regulations demanded that he should be sent down into the cells reserved for insubordinate prisoners. "M. Berryer came again to lighten my woes; outside the prison he demanded justice and mercy for me, inside he sought to calm my grief, which seemed less poignant when he assured me that he shared it." The lieutenant of police ordered the prisoner to be fed as well as formerly, and to be allowed his books, papers, knick-knacks, and the privilege of the two hours' walk he had enjoyed at Vincennes. In return for these kindnesses, the assistant surgeon sent to the magistrate "a remedy for the gout." He asked at the same time to be allowed to breed little birds, whose chirping and lively movements would divert him. The request was granted. But instead of bearing his lot with patience, Danry grew more and more irritable every day. He gave free rein to his violent temper, raised a hubbub, shrieked, tore up and down his room, so that they came perforce to believe that he was going mad. On the books of the Bastille library, which circulated from room to room, he wrote ribald verses against the Marquise de Pompadour.

In this way he prolonged his sojourn in the cells. Gradually his letters changed their tone. "It is a little hard to be left for fourteen months in prison, a whole year of the time, ending to-day, in one cell where I still am."

Then Berryer put him back into a good room, about the end of the year 1751. At the same time he gave him, at the king's expense, a servant to wait on him.

As to Annette Benoist, she had been set at liberty after a fortnight's detention. Danry's servant fell sick; as there was no desire to deprive the prisoner of society, he was given a companion. This was a certain Antoine Allègre, who had been there since May 29, 1750. The circumstances which had led to his imprisonment were almost identical with those to which Danry owed his confinement. Allègre was keeping a school at Marseilles when he learnt that the enemies of the Marquise de Pompadour were seeking to destroy her. He fabricated a story of a conspiracy in which he involved Maurepas, the Archbishop of Albi, and the Bishop of Lodève; he sent a denunciation of this plot to Versailles, and, to give it some semblance of truth, addressed to the favourite's valet a letter in disguised handwriting, beginning with these words: "On the word of a gentleman, there are 100,000 crowns for you if you poison your mistress." He hoped by this means to obtain a good situation, or the success of a business project he had in hand.

Intelligent, with some education, and venturesome,

Danry and Allègre were just the men to get on well together, so much the better that the schoolmaster dominated the comrade to whom he was so much superior. The years that Danry spent in company with Allègre exercised so great an influence on his whole life that the lieutenant of police, Lenoir, could say one day : " Danry is the second volume of Allègre." The letters of the latter, a large number of which have been preserved, bear witness to the originality and energy of his mind : their style is fine and fluent, of the purest French ; the ideas expressed have distinction and are sometimes remarkable without eccentricity. He worked untiringly, and was at first annoyed at the presence of a companion : " Give me, I beg you, a room to myself," he wrote to Berryer, " even without a fire : I like being alone, I am sufficient for myself, because I can find things to do, and seed to sow for the future." His temperament was naturally mystical, but of that cold and acrid mysticism which we sometimes find in men of science, and mathematicians in particular. For Allègre's principal studies were mathematics, mechanics, and engineering. The lieutenant of police procured for him works on fortification, architecture, mechanics, hydraulics. The prisoner used them to compile essays on the most diverse questions, which he sent to the lieutenant of police in the hope of their procuring his liberation. Those essays which we possess show the extent of his intelligence and his education. Danry followed his example by-and-by, in this as in everything else, but clumsily. Allègre was also very clever with his fingers, and could make, so the officials of the château declared, whatever he pleased.

Allègre was a dangerous man : the warders were afraid of him. Some time after his entrance into the Bastille he fell ill, and a man was set to look after him ; the two men did not agree at all. Allègre sent complaint after complaint to the lieutenant of police. An inquiry was made which turned out not unfavourable to the keeper, and he was left with the prisoner. One morning—September 8, 1751—the officers of the Bastille heard cries and clamour in the " Well " tower. Hastily ascending, they found Allègre in the act of stabbing his companion, who lay on the floor held down by the throat, wallowing in the blood that streamed from a gash in the stomach. If Allègre had not been in the Bastille, the Parlement would have had him broken on the wheel in the Place de Grève : the Bastille was his safety, though he could no longer hope for a speedy liberation.

Danry, in his turn, wore out the patience of his guardians. Major Chevalier, who was kindness itself, wrote to the lieutenant of police : " He is no better than Allègre, but though more turbulent and choleric, he is much less to be feared in every respect." The physician of the Bastille, Dr. Boyer, a member of the Academy, wrote likewise : " I have good reason to distrust the man." The temper of Danry became embittered. He began to revile the warders. One morning they were obliged to take from him a knife and other sharp instruments he had concealed. He used the paper they gave him to open communications with other prisoners and with people outside. Paper was withheld: he then wrote with his blood on a handkerchief; he was forbidden by the lieutenant of police to write to him with his blood, so he wrote on tablets made of bread crumbs, which he passed out secretly between two plates.

The use of paper was then restored to him, which did not prevent him from writing to Berryer: "My lord, I am writing to you with my blood on linen, because the officers refuse me ink and paper; it is now more than six times that I have asked in vain to speak to them. What are you about, my lord? Do not drive me to extremities. At least, do not force me to be my own executioner. Send a sentry to break my head for me; that is the very least favour you can do me." Berryer, astonished at this missive, remarked on it to the major, who replied: "I have not refused paper to Danry."

So the prisoner forced them more and more to the conclusion that he was a madman. On October 13, 1753, he wrote to Dr. Quesnay to tell him that he wished him well, but that being too poor to give him anything else, he was making him a present of his body, which was on the point of perishing, for him to make a skeleton of. To the paper on which he wrote, Danry had sewn a little square of cloth, adding: "God has given the garments of martyrs the virtue of healing all manner of diseases. It is now fifty-seven months since I have been suffering an enforced martyrdom. So there is no

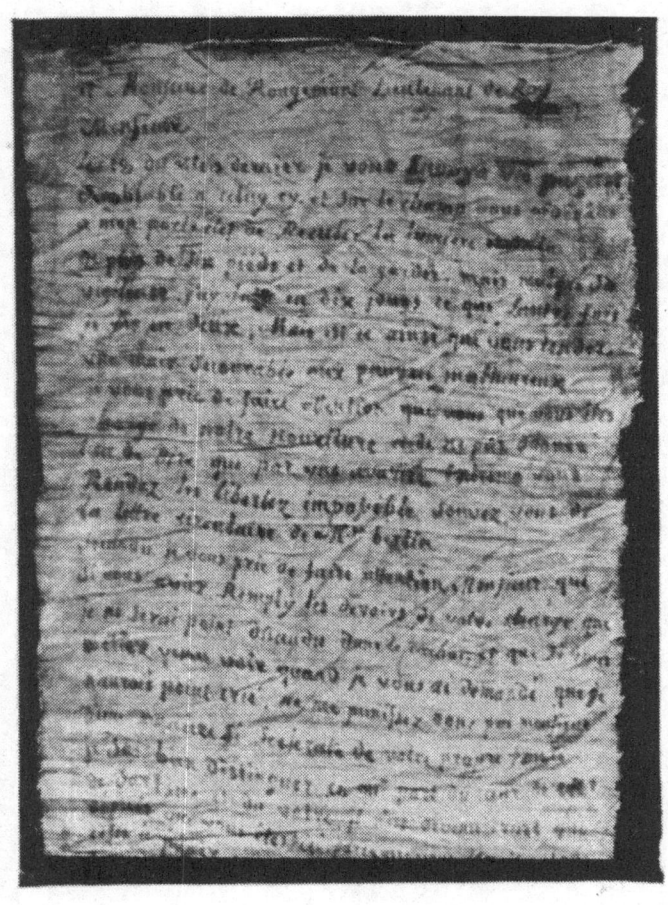

Beginning of a letter written with blood on linen by Danry (Latude), while a prisoner at Vincennes, to Rougemont, the king's lieutenant.

doubt that to-day the cloth of my coat will work miracles; here is a bit for you." This letter was returned to the lieutenant of police in December, and on it we find a marginal note in Berryer's hand: "A letter worth keeping, as it reveals the prisoner's mind." We know in what fashion madmen were wont to be treated in the eighteenth century.

But suddenly, to the great astonishment of the officers of the château, our two friends amended their character and their conduct. No more noises were heard in their room, and they answered politely anyone who came to speak to them. But their behaviour was even more odd than ever. Allègre used to walk up and down the room half naked, "to save his toggery," he said, and he sent letter after letter to his brother and the lieutenant of police, asking them to send him things, particularly shirts and handkerchiefs. Danry followed suit. "This prisoner," wrote Chevalier to the lieutenant of police, "is asking for linen. I shall not make a requisition, because he has seven very good shirts, four of them new; he has shirts on the brain." But why decline to humour a prisoner's whim? So the commissary of the Bastille had two dozen expensive shirts made—every one cost twenty livres, more than thirty-three shillings of our money—and some handkerchiefs of the finest cambric.

If the wardrobe-keeper of the Bastille had kept her eyes open, she would have noticed that the serviettes and cloths which went into the room of the two companions were of much smaller dimensions when they came out. Our friends had established communication with their neighbours above and below, begging twine and thread from them and giving tobacco in exchange. They had succeeded in loosening the iron bars which prevented climbing up the chimney; at night they used to mount to the platforms, whence they conversed down the chimneys with prisoners in the other towers. One of these hapless creatures believed himself to be a prophet of God; he heard at night the sound of a voice descending upon his cold hearth: he revealed the miracle to the officers, who only considered him still more insane than before. On the terrace Allègre and Danry found the tools left there in the evening by the masons and gardeners employed at the Bastille. Thus they got possession of a mallet, an auger, two sorts of pulleys, and some bits of iron taken from the gun-carriages. All these they concealed in the hollow between the floor of their room and the ceiling of the room below.

Allègre and Danry escaped from the Bastille on the night of February 25, 1756. They climbed up the chimney till they reached the platform, and descended by means of their famous rope ladder, fastened to a gun-carriage. A wall separated the Bastille moat from that of the Arsenal. By the aid of an iron bar they succeeded in working out a large stone, and they escaped through the hole thus made. Their rope ladder was a work of long patience and amazing skill. When in after days Allègre went mad, Danry appropriated the whole credit of this enterprise which his friend had conceived and directed.

At the moment of leaving, Allègre had written on a scrap of paper, for the officers of the Bastille, the following note, which is an excellent indication of his character:—

"We have done no damage to the furniture of the governor, we have only made use of a few rags of coverlets of no possible use; the others are left just as they were. If some serviettes are missing, they will be found at the bottom of the water in the great moat, whither we are taking them to wipe our feet.

"*Non nobis, Domine, non nobis, sed nomini tuo da gloriam!*

"*Scito cor nostrum et cognosce semitas nostras.*"[1]

Our two companions had provided themselves with a portmanteau, and they made haste to change their clothes as soon as they had cleared the precincts of the fortress. A foreman of works whom Danry knew interested himself in them, and conducted them to one Rouit, a tailor, who lodged them for some little time. Rouit even lent Danry forty-eight livres, which he promised to return as soon as he reached Brussels. At the end of a month our two friends were across the frontier.

It is very difficult to follow Danry's proceedings from the time when he left Rouit to the moment of his re-

---

[1] "Not unto us, O Lord, but unto Thy name give glory!
"Know our heart and search out our ways."

incarceration in the Bastille. He has left, it is true, two accounts of his sojourn in Flanders and Holland; but these accounts are themselves inconsistent, and both differ from some original documents which remain to us.

The two fugitives had considered it advisable not to set out together. Allègre was the first to arrive at Brussels, whence he wrote an insolent letter to Madame de Pompadour. This letter led to his discovery. On reaching Brussels, Danry learnt that his friend had been arrested. He lost no time in making for Holland, and at Amsterdam he took service with one Paul Melenteau. From Rotterdam he had written to his mother, and the poor creature, collecting her little savings, sent him 200 livres by post. But Saint-Marc had already struck on the track of the fugitive. "The burgomaster of Amsterdam readily and gladly granted the request made by Saint-Marc on behalf of the king, through the ambassador, for the arrest and extradition of Danry." Louis XV. confined himself to claiming him as one of his subjects. Saint-Marc, disguised as an Armenian merchant, discovered him in his retreat. Danry was arrested in Amsterdam on June 1, 1756, conducted to a cell belonging to the town hall, and thence brought back to France and consigned to the Bastille on June 9. Word came from Holland that Saint-Marc was there regarded as a sorcerer.

By his second escape the unhappy man had succeeded in making his case very serious. In the eighteenth century, escape from a state prison was punishable with death. The English, great apostles of humanity as they were, were no more lenient than the French; and everyone knows what treatment was meted out by Frederick II. to Baron de Trenck. He was to have remained in prison only one year; but after his second escape he was chained up in a gloomy dungeon; at his feet was the grave in which he was to be buried, and on it his name and a death's-head had been cut.

The government of Louis XV. did not punish with such rigour as this. The fugitive was simply put in the cells for a time. At the Bastille the cells were damp and chilly dungeons. Danry has left in his *Memoirs* an account of the forty months spent in this dismal place,—an account which makes one's hair stand on end; but it is packed full of exaggeration. He says that he spent three years with irons on his hands and feet: in November, 1756, Berryer offered to remove the irons from either hands or feet at his choice, and we see from a marginal note by Major Chevalier that he chose the feet. Danry adds that he lay all through the winter on straw without any coverlet: he was actually so well supplied with coverlets that he applied to Berryer for some others. To believe him you would think that when the Seine was in flood the water rose as high as his waist: as a fact, when the water threatened to invade the cell, the prisoner was removed. Again, he says that he passed there forty months in absolute darkness: the light of his prison was certainly not very brilliant, but it was sufficient to enable him to read and write, and we learn from letters he sent to the lieutenant of police that he saw from his cell all that went on in the courtyard of the Bastille. Finally, he tells us of a variety of diseases he contracted at the time, and cites in this connection the opinion of an oculist who came to attend him. But this very report was forged by Danry himself, and the rest he invented to match.

In this cell, where he professes to have been treated in so barbarous a manner, Danry, however, proved difficult enough to deal with, as we judge from the reports of Chevalier. "Danry has a thoroughly nasty temper; he sends for us at eight o'clock in the morning, and asks us to send warders to the market to buy him fish, saying that he never eats eggs, artichokes, or spinach, and that he insists on eating fish; and when we refuse, he flies into a furious passion." That was on fast days; on ordinary days it was the same. "Danry swore like a trooper, that is, in his usual way, and after the performance said to me: 'Major, when you give me a fowl, at least let it be stuffed!'" He was not one of the vulgar herd, he said, "one of those fellows you send to Bicêtre." And he demanded to be treated in a manner befitting his condition.

It was just the same with regard to clothes. One is amazed at the sight of the lists of things the lieutenant of police got made for him. To give him satisfaction, the administration did not stick at the most unreasonable expense, and it was by selling these clothes that Danry, at his various escapes, procured a part of the money he was so much in need of. He suffered from rheumatism, so they provided him with dressing-gowns lined with rabbit-skin, vests lined with silk plush, gloves and fur hats, and first-rate leather breeches. In his *Memoirs* Danry lumps all these as "half-rotten rags." Rochebrune, the commissary charged with the prisoners' supplies, was quite unable to satisfy him. "You instructed me," he wrote to the major, "to get a dressing-gown made for the Sieur Danry, who asks for a calamanco with red stripes on a blue ground. I have made inquiries for such stuff of a dozen tradesmen, who have no such thing, and indeed would be precious careful not to have it, for there is no sale for that kind of calamanco. I don't see why I should satisfy the fantastic tastes of a prisoner who ought to be very well pleased at having a dressing-gown that is warm and well-fitting." On another occasion, the major writes: "This man Danry has never up to the present consented to accept the breeches that M. de Rochebrune got made for him, though they are excellent, lined with good leather, with silk garters, and in the best style." And Danry had his own pretty way of complaining. "I beg you," he wrote to the governor, "to have the goodness to tell M. de Sartine in plain terms that the four handkerchiefs he sent me are not fit to give to a galley-slave, and I will not have them on any account; but that I request him kindly to give me six print handkerchiefs, blue, and large, and two muslin cravats." He adds, "If there is no money in the treasury, go and ask Madame de Pompadour for some."

One day Danry declared that something was wrong with his eyes. Grandjean, the king's oculist, came more than once to see him, ordered aromatic fumigations for him, gave him ointments and eye-salve; but it was soon seen that all that was wrong was that Danry desired to get a spy-glass, and to smuggle out, with the doctor's assistance, memoirs and letters.

On September 1, 1759, Danry was removed from the cells and placed in a more airy chamber. He wrote at once to Bertin to thank him, and to tell him that he was sending him two doves. "You delight in doing good, and I shall have no less delight, my lord, if you favour me by accepting this slight mark of my great gratitude.

"Tamerlaine allowed himself to be disarmed by a basket of figs presented to him by the inhabitants of a town he was proceeding to besiege. The Marquise de Pompadour is a Christian lady; I beg you to allow me to send her also a pair: perhaps she will allow her heart to be touched by these two innocent pigeons. I append a copy of the letter which will accompany them :—

"'MADAM,—Two pigeons used to come every day to pick grains out of my straw; I kept them, and they gave me young ones. I venture to take the liberty of presenting you with this pair as a mark of my respect and affection. I beseech you in mercy to be good enough to accept them, with as much pleasure as I have in offering them to you. I have the honour to be, with the profoundest respect, Madam, your very humble and obedient servant,

"' DANRY, for eleven years at the Bastille.'"

Why did not Danry always make so charming a use of the permission accorded him to write to the minister, the lieutenant of police, Madame de Pompadour, Dr. Quesnay, and his mother? He wrote incessantly, and we have letters of his in hundreds, widely differing one from another. Some are suppliant and pathetic: "My body is wasting away every day in tears and blood, I am worn out." He writes to Madame de Pompadour:—"Madam,—I have never wished you anything but well; be then sensible to the voice of tears, of my innocence, and of a poor despairing mother of sixty-six years. Madam, you are well aware of my martyrdom. I beg you in God's name to grant me my precious liberty; I am spent, I am dying, my blood is all on fire by reason of my groaning; twenty times in the night I am obliged to moisten my mouth and nostrils to get my breath." Everyone knows the famous letter beginning with the words, "I have been suffering now for 100,000 hours." He writes to Quesnay: "I present myself to you with a live coal upon my head, indicating my pressing necessity." The images he uses are not always so happy: "Listen," he says to Berryer, "to the voice of the just bowels with which you are arrayed"!

In other letters the prisoner alters his tone; to plaints

succeed cries of rage and fury, "he steeps his pen in the gall with which his soul is saturated." He no longer supplicates, he threatens. There is nothing to praise in the style of these epistles : it is incorrect and vulgar, though at times vigorous and coloured with vivid imagery. To the lieutenant of police he writes : "When a man is to be punished in this accursed prison, the air is full of it, the punishments fall quicker than the thunderbolt ; but when it is a case of succouring a man who is unfortunate, I see nothing but crabs ; " and he addresses to him these lines of Voltaire :—

> "Perish those villains born, whose hearts of steel
> No touch of ruth for others' woes can feel."

He predicts terrible retribution for the ministers, the magistrates, and Madame de Pompadour. To her he writes : "You will see yourself one day like that owl in the park of Versailles; all the birds cast water upon him to choke him, to drown him; if the king chanced to die, before two hours were past someone would set five or six persons at your heels, and you would yourself pack to the Bastille." The accused by degrees becomes transformed into the accuser ; he writes to Sartine : "I am neither a dog nor a criminal, but a man like yourself." And the lieutenant of police, taking pity on him, writes on one of these letters sent to the minister of Paris : "When Danry writes thus, it is not that he is mad, but frantic from long imprisonment." The magistrate counsels the prisoner "to keep out of his letters all bitterness, which can only do him harm." Bertin corrected with his own hand the petitions Danry sent to the Marquise de Pompadour; in the margin of one of them we read, "I should think I was prejudicing him and his interests if I sent on to Madame de Pompadour a letter in which he ventures to reproach her with having *abused his good faith and confidence*." Having amended the letter, the lieutenant of police himself carried it to Versailles.

The years of captivity, far from humbling the prisoner and abasing his pride, only made him the more arrogant; his audacity grew from day to day, and he was not afraid of speaking to the lieutenants of police themselves, who knew his history, about his fortune which had been ruined, his brilliant career which had been cut short, his whole family plunged into despair. At first the magistrate would shrug his shoulders; insensibly he would be won over by these unwavering assertions, by this accent of conviction; and he ends actually by believing in this high birth, this fortune, this genius, in all which Danry had perhaps come to believe himself. Then Danry takes a still higher tone: he claims not only his freedom, but compensation, large sums of money, honours. But one must not think that this sprang from a sordid sentiment unworthy of him: "If I propose compensation, my lord, it is not for the sake of getting money, it is only so that I may smooth away all the obstacles which may delay the end of my long suffering."

In return, he is very ready to give the lieutenant of

police some good advice—to indicate the means of advancement in his career, to show him how to set about getting appointed secretary of state, to compose for him the speech he is to make to the king at his first audience. He adds: "This very time is extremely favourable to you; it is the auspicious hour: profit by it. Before they take horse on the day of rejoicing for the conclusion of peace, you ought to be a counsellor of state."

He is very ready also to send to the king schemes conceived in his prison for the welfare of the realm. Now it is a suggestion to give sergeants and officers on the battlefield muskets instead of spontoons and pikes, by which the French arms would be strengthened by 25,000 good fusiliers. Now it is a suggestion for increasing postal facilities, which would augment the resources of the Treasury by several millions every year. He recommends the erection of public granaries in the principal towns, and draws up plans of battle for giving unheard-of strength to a column of men three deep. We might mention other and better suggestions. These notions were drowned in a flood of words, an unimaginable wealth of verbiage, with parallels drawn from the history of all periods and every country. His manuscripts were illustrated with pen and ink sketches. Danry copied and recopied them incessantly, sent them to all and sundry in all sorts of forms, persuaded the sentinels that these lofty conceptions intimately concerned the safety of the state and would win him an immense fortune. Thus he induced these good fellows to compromise their situation by carrying the papers secretly to ministers, members of the Parlement, marshals of France ; he threw them from the windows of his room, and, wrapped in snowballs, from the top of the towers. These memoirs are the work of a man whose open and active mind, of incredible activity indeed, plans, constructs, invents without cessation or repose.

Among these bundles of papers we have discovered a very touching letter from the prisoner's mother, Jeanneton Aubrespy, who wrote to her son from Montagnac on June 14, 1759 :—

"Do not do me the injustice of thinking that I have forgotten you, my dear son, my loving son. Could I shut you out of my thoughts, you whom I bear always in my heart ? I have always had a great longing to see you again, but to-day I long more than ever, I am constantly concerned for you, I think of nothing but you, I am wholly filled with you. Do not worry, my dear son ; that is the only favour I ask of you. Your misfortunes will come to an end, and perhaps it is not far off. I hope that Madame de Pompadour will pardon you ; for that I am trying to win heaven and earth over to your cause. The Lord is putting my submission and yours to a long test, so as to make us better realize the worth of His favour. Do not distress yourself, my son. I hope to have the happiness of receiving you again, and of embracing you more tenderly than ever. Adieu, my son, my dear son, my loving son, I love you, and I shall love you dearly to the grave. I beg you to give me news of your health. I am, and always shall be, your good mother, DAUBRESPI, *widow*."

Is not this letter charming in its artless pathos? The son's reply is equally touching; but on reading it again one feels that it was to pass under the eyes of the lieutenant of police; on examining it closely, one sees the sentiments grimacing between the lines.

No one knew better than Danry how to play on the souls of others, to awake in them, at his will, pity or tenderness, astonishment or admiration. No one has surpassed him in the art, difficult in very truth, of posing as a hero, a genius, and a martyr, a part that we shall see him sustain for twenty years without faltering.

In 1759 there entered upon the office of lieutenant of police a man who was henceforth to occupy Danry's mind almost exclusively—Gabriel de Sartine. He was a fine sceptic, of amiable character and pleasing manners. He was loved by the people of Paris, who boasted of his administrative abilities and his spirit of justice. He exerted himself in his turn to render the years of captivity less cruel to Danry. "He allowed me," writes the latter, "what no other State prisoner has ever obtained, the privilege of walking along the top of the towers, in the open air, to preserve my health." He cheered the prisoner with genial words, and urged him to behave well and no longer to fill his letters with insults.

"Your fate," he told him, "is in your own hands." He looked into Danry's scheme for the construction of public granaries, and when he had read it said, "Really, there are excellent things, most excellent things in it." He visited Danry in prison and promised to do his utmost to obtain his liberation. He himself put into the hands of Madame de Pompadour the *Grand Mémoire* which Danry had drawn up for her. In this memorial the prisoner told the favourite that in return for a service he had rendered her in sending her a "hieroglyphic symbol" to put her on her guard against the machinations of her enemies, she had caused him to suffer unjustly for twelve years. Moreover, he would now only accept his freedom along with an indemnity of 60,000 livres. He added: "Be on your guard! When your prisoners get out and publish your cruelties abroad, they will make you hateful to heaven and the whole earth!" It is not surprising that this *Grand Mémoire* had practically no result. Sartine promised that he would renew his efforts on his behalf. "If, unhappily, you should meet with some resistance to the entreaties you are about to make for me," wrote Danry, "I take the precaution of sending you a copy of the scheme I sent to the king." (This was the memorial suggesting that muskets should be given to the officers and sergeants.) "Now the king has been putting my scheme in operation for five years or more, and he will continue to avail himself of it every time we are at war." Sartine proceeded to Versailles, this marvellous scheme in his pocket. He showed it to the ministers and pleaded on behalf of this protégé of his who, from the depths of his dungeon, was doing his country service. But on his return he wrote to the major of the Bastille a note in regard to Danry, in which we read: "They have not made use, as he believes, of his military scheme."

Danry had asked several times to be sent to the colonies. In 1763 the government was largely occupied with the colonization of La Désirade. We find a letter of June 23, 1763, in which Sartine proposes to send Danry to La Désirade "with an introduction to the commanding officer." But nothing came of these proposals.

All his life, Danry sought to compass his ends by the aid of women. He was well aware of all the tenderness and devotion there is in these light heads; he knew that sentiment is always stronger in them than reason: "I was always looking out for women, and wished to find young women, for their gentle and loving soul is more susceptible of pity; misfortune moves them, stirs in them a more lively interest; their impressionability is less quickly dulled, and so they are capable of greater efforts."

While taking his walk on the towers of the Bastille in the fresh morning air, he tried by means of gestures and signals to open relations with the people of the neighbourhood. "One day I noticed two young persons working alone in a room, whose countenances struck me as pretty and gentle. I was not deceived. One of them having glanced in my direction, I wafted her with my hand a salutation which I endeavoured to make respectful and becoming, whereupon she told her sister, who instantly looked at me too. I then saluted them both in the same manner, and they replied to me with an appearance of interest and kindliness. From that moment we set up a sort of correspondence between us." The girls were two good-looking laundresses named Lebrun, the daughters of a wigmaker. And our rogue, the better to stimulate the little fools to enthusiastic service in his behalf, knocked at the door of their young hearts, willing enough to fly open. He spoke to them of youth, misfortune, love—and also of his fortune, prodigious, he said, the half of which he offered them. Glowing with ardour, the girls spared for him neither time, nor trouble, nor what little money they had.

The prisoner had put them in possession of several of his schemes, among others the military one, with letters for certain writers and persons of importance, and in addition a "terrible" indictment of Madame de Pompadour for the king, in which "her birth and her shame, all her thefts and cruelties were laid bare." He begged the girls to have several copies made, which they were then to send to the addresses indicated. Soon large black crosses daubed on a neighbouring wall informed the prisoner that his instructions had been carried out. Danry seems no longer to have doubted that his woes were coming to an end, that the gates of the Bastille were about to fly open before him, and that he would triumphantly leave the prison only to enter a palace of fortune: *Parta victoria!*[1] he exclaims in a burst of happiness.

And so we come to one of the most extraordinary episodes in this strange life.

In December, 1763, the Marquise of Pompadour was taken seriously ill. "An officer of the Bastille came up to my room and said to me: 'Sir, write four words to the Marquise de Pompadour, and you may be sure that in less than a week you will have recovered your freedom.' I replied to the major that prayers and tears only hardened the heart of that cruel woman, and that I would not write to her. However, he came back next day with the same story, and I replied in the same terms as on the previous day. Scarcely had he gone than Daragon, my warder, came into my room and said: 'Believe the major when he tells you that within a week you will be free: if he tells you so, depend upon it he is sure of it.' Next day but one the officer came to me for the third time: 'Why are you so obstinate?' I thanked him—it was Chevalier, major of the Bastille—for the third time, telling him that I would sooner die than write again to that implacable shrew.

"Six or eight days after, my two young ladies came and kissed their hands to me, at the same time displaying a roll of paper on which were written in large characters the words: 'Madame de Pompadour is dead!' The

[1] "The victory is won!"—T.

Marquise de Pompadour died on April 19, 1764, and two months afterwards, on June 19, M. de Sartine came to the Bastille and gave me an audience; the first thing he said was that we would say no more about the past, but that at the earliest moment he would go to Versailles and demand of the minister the justice which was my due." And we find, in truth, among the papers of the lieutenant of police, the following note, dated June 18, 1764: "M. Duval (one of the lieutenant's secretaries)—to propose at the first inspection that Danry be liberated and exiled to his own part of the country."

Returning to his room, Danry reflected on these developments; for the lieutenant of police to show so much anxiety for his liberation was evidently a sign that he was afraid of him, and that his memorials had reached their destination and achieved their end. But he would be a great ass to be satisfied with a mere liberation: "100,000 livres" would scarcely suffice to throw oblivion over the injustices with which he had been overwhelmed.

He revolved these thoughts in his head for several days. To accept freedom at the hands of his persecutors would be to pardon the past, a mistake he would never fall into. The door opened, the major entered, bearing in his hand a note written by de Sartine: "You will tell County Number 4 that I am working for his effectual liberation." The officer went out; Danry immediately sat down at his table and wrote to the lieutenant of police a letter replete with threats, insults, and obscenity.

The original is lost, but we have an abstract made by Danry himself. He concluded with leaving to Sartine a choice: " he was either a mere lunatic, or else had allowed himself to be corrupted like a villain by the gold of the Marquis de Marigny, the Marquise de Pompadour's brother."

"When Sartine received my letter, he wrote an answer which the major brought and read to me, in which these were his very words: that I was wrong to impute to him the length of my imprisonment, that if he had had his way I should long ago have been set free; and he ended by telling me that there was Bedlam for the mad. On which I said to the major: 'We shall see in a few days whether he will have the power to put me in Bedlam.' He did not deprive me of my walk on the towers; nine days after, he put me in the cells on bread and water." But Danry was not easily put out. No doubt they were only meaning to put his assurance to the test. He went down to his cell singing, and for several days continued to manifest the most confident gaiety.

From that moment the prisoner made himself insufferable to his guardians. It was yells and violence from morning to night. He filled the whole Bastille with bursts of his " voice of thunder." Major Chevalier wrote to Sartine: " This prisoner would wear out the patience of the saintliest monk "; again: " He is full of gall and bitterness, he is poison pure and simple "; once more: " This prisoner is raving mad."

The lieutenant of police suggested to Saint-Florentin, the minister, to transfer Danry to the keep of Vincennes. He was conducted there on the night of September 15, 1764. We are now entering on a new phase of his life. We shall find him still more wretched than in the past, but constantly swelling his demands and pretensions, and with reason, for he is now, mark you, a nobleman ! He had learnt from a sentinel of the Bastille of the death of Henri Vissec de la Tude, lieutenant-colonel of a dragoon regiment, who had died at Sedan on January 31, 1761. From that day he determined that he was the son of that officer. And what were his reasons? Vissec de la Tude was from his own part of the country, he was a nobleman and rich, and he was dead. These arguments Danry considered excellent. He was, however, in complete ignorance of all that concerned his father and his new family; he did not know even the name "Vissec de la Tude," of which he made "Masers de la Tude"; Masers was the name of an estate belonging to Baron de Fontès, a relation of Henri de Vissec. The latter was not a marquis, as Danry believed, but simply a chevalier; he died leaving six sons, whilst Danry represents him as dying without issue. It goes without saying that all that our hero relates about his father in his *Memoirs* is pure invention. The Chevalier de la Tude never knew of the existence of the son of Jeanneton Aubrespy, and when in later years Danry asked the children to recognize him as their natural brother, his pretensions were rejected. Nevertheless our gentleman will henceforth sign his letters and memoirs "Danry, or rather Henri Masers d'Aubrespy," then "de Masers d'Aubrespy," then "de Masers de la Tude." When Danry had once got an idea in his head, he never let it go. He repeated it unceasingly until he had forced it upon the conviction of all about him—pertinacity which cannot fail to excite our admiration. In the patent of Danry's pension of 400 livres granted by Louis XVI. in 1784, the king calls the son of poor Jeanneton " Vicomte Masers de la Tude."

As may well be imagined, the Vicomte de la Tude could not accept his liberty on the same terms as Danry. The latter would have been satisfied with 60,000 livres: the viscount demands 150,000 and the cross of St. Louis to boot. So he writes to the lieutenant of police. Sartine was too sensible a man to be long obdurate to the prisoner on account of these extravagances. "I was transferred to the keep of Vincennes on the night of September 15, 1764. About nine hours after, the late M. de Guyonnet, king's lieutenant, came and saw me in the presence of the major and the three warders, and said : ' M. de Sartine has instructed me to inform you, on his behalf, that provided you behave yourself quietly for a short time, he will set you free. You have written him a very violent letter, and you must apologize for it.'" Danry adds : "When all is said and done, M. de Sartine did treat me well." He granted him for two hours every day "the extraordinary promenade of the moats." "When a lieutenant of police," says Danry, "granted this privilege to a prisoner, it was with the object of promptly setting him free." On November 23, 1765, Danry was walking thus, in company with a sentinel, outside the keep. The fog was dense. Turning suddenly towards his keeper, Danry said, "What do you think of this weather?" "It's very bad." "Well, it's just the weather to escape in." He took five paces and was out of sight. "I escaped from Vincennes," writes Danry, "without trickery; an ox would have managed it as well." But in the speech he delivered later in the National Assembly, the matter took a new complexion. "Think," he cried, "of the unfortunate Latude, in his third escape, pursued by twenty soldiers, and yet stopping and disarming under their very eyes the sentinel who had taken aim at him!"

When Latude was at large, he found himself without resources, as at his first escape. "I escaped with my feet in slippers and not a sou in my pocket; I hadn't a thing to bless myself with." He took refuge with his young friends, the Misses Lebrun.

In their keeping he found a part of his papers, plans and projects, memorials and dissertations. He sent "a basketful" of these to Marshal de Noailles, begging him to continue to honour him with his protection, and imparting to him "four great discoveries he had just made; first, the true cause of the tides; secondly, the true cause of mountains, but for which the globe would be brought to a standstill and become speedily vitrified; thirdly, the cause of the ceaseless turning of the globe; fourthly, the cause of the saltness of sea-water." He wrote also to the Duke de Choiseul, minister of war, in order to obtain a reward for his military scheme; he wrote making overtures of peace to Sartine: in return for an advance of 10,000 crowns of the 150,000 livres due to him, he would overlook the past: "I was resolved," he says, "to stake all on one cast." In reply, he received a letter naming a house where he would find 1200 livres obtained for him by Dr. Quesnay. He proceeded to the address indicated—and was there captured.

He was at once taken back to Vincennes. He declares that he was about to be set at liberty at the moment of his escape: and now a new detention was commencing. We shall not relate in detail the life he was now to lead. Materially he continued to be well treated, but his mind became affected, his rages became more and more violent, reaching at last paroxysms of fury. Here are some extracts from letters and memorials sent to Sartine: "By all the devils, this is coming it too strong. It is true, sir, that I'd defy the blackest devils in all hell to teach you anything in the way of cruelty; and that's but poor praise for you." He writes on another occasion: "The crime of every one of us is to have seen through your villainies: we are to perish, are we? how delighted you would be if some one told you that we had all strangled ourselves in our cells!" Danry reminds the lieutenant of police of the tortures of Enguerrand de Marigni, adding:

"Remember that more than a thousand wretches have been broken in the Place de Grève who had not committed the hundredth part of your crimes." . . . . "Not a single person would be astonished to see you flayed alive, your skin tanned, and your carcase thrown into the gutters for the dogs to eat." . . . "But Monsieur laughs at everything, Monsieur fears neither God, nor king, nor devil, Monsieur swills down his crimes like buttermilk!"

In prison Latude wrote memoirs which he filled with calumnies on the ministers and the court. These memoirs are composed in the most dramatic style, with an inimitable accent of sincerity. It was known that the prisoner found a thousand means of sending them outside the walls, and it was feared that they might be circulated among the populace, whose minds—the year is 1775—were beginning to ferment. Latude had just been flung into a cell in consequence of a fresh outbreak against his jailers. "On March 19, 1775, the king's lieutenant entered, accompanied by the major and three warders, and said to me: 'I have obtained leave to let you out of the cell, but on one condition: that you hand over your papers.'

"'Hand over my papers! I tell you, sir, I'd rather be done to death in this cell than show the white feather so!'

"'Your trunk is upstairs in your room: I've only to say the word and the seals would be broken and your papers taken out.'

"I replied: 'Sir, justice has formalities to which you are bound to conform, and you are not allowed to commit such outrages.'

"He took five or six steps out of the cell, and as I did not call him back, he came back himself and said: 'Just hand them to me for ten days to examine them, and I give you my word of honour that at the end of that time I will have them returned to your room.'

"I replied: 'I will not let you have them for two hours even.'

"'All right,' he said; 'as you won't entrust them to me, you have only to stay where you are.'"

Latude relates in his *Memoirs* with great indignation the story of a flute he had made, on which he used to play, his sole diversion during the long hours of solitude; his jailers had the barbarity to take it from him. The governor of the fortress, out of compassion, offered to restore it. "But it will only be on condition that you play by day only, and not at night." At this stipulation, writes Latude in his *Rêveries*, "I could not refrain from bantering him, saying, 'Why, don't you know, sir, that forbidding a thing is just the way to make me eager for it?'"

And so at Vincennes as at Paris they came to consider Danry as a madman. Among the books given him for his amusement there were some dealing with sorcery. These he read and re-read, and from that time onward he saw in all the incidents of his life nothing but the perpetual intervention of devils evoked by the witch

Madame de Pompadour and her brother the magician, the Marquis de Marigny.

Sartine came again to see the prisoner on November 8, 1772. Danry begged him to send a police officer to make a copy of a memorial he had drawn up for his own justification; to send also an advocate to assist him with his advice, and a doctor, to examine the state of his health. The police officer arrived on the 24th. On the 29th, he wrote to the lieutenant of police: "I have the honour to report that in pursuance of your orders I proceeded to the château of Vincennes on the 24th curt., to hear from Danry something which, he asserts, concerns the minister: it is impossible to hear anything which concerns him less. He began by saying that to write all he had to tell me I should have to remain for three weeks with him. He was bound to tell me the story of 180 sorceries, and I was to copy the story, according to him, from a heap of papers he drew from a bag, the writing of which is undecipherable."

We know from Danry himself what passed at the visit of the advocate. He entered the prisoner's room about noon. Danry handed him two memorials he had drawn up and explained their purport. "Instantly he cut me short, saying, 'Sir, I have no belief whatever in witchcraft.' I did not give in, but said, 'Sir, I cannot show you the devil in bodily shape, but I am very certain I can convince you, by the contents of this memorial, that the late Marquise de Pompadour was a witch, and that the Marquis de Marigny, her brother, is at this very time still having dealings with the devil.'

"The advocate had read but a few pages when he stopped dead, put the manuscript on the table, and said, as though he had been wakened out of a deep sleep, 'Would you not like to get out of prison?' I replied: 'There's no doubt of that.' 'And do you intend to remain in Paris, or to go to your home?' 'When I am free, I shall go home.' 'But have you any means?' Upon this I took his hand and said: 'My dear sir, I beg you not to take offence at what I am going to say.' 'Speak on,' he said, 'say whatever you like, I shall not be offended.' 'Well then, I see very clearly that the devil has already got hold of you.'"

In the same year, Malesherbes made his celebrated inspection of the prisons. "This virtuous minister came to see me at the beginning of August, 1775, and listened to me with the most lively interest." The historian who has the completest knowledge of everything relating to the Bastille, François Ravaisson, believed that Malesherbes left the wretched man in prison out of regard for his colleague Maurepas. "One would have thought that Maurepas' first act on resuming office would have been to release his old accomplice." This conjecture is destroyed by a letter from Malesherbes to the governor of Vincennes: "I am busy, sir, with the examination of the papers relating to your various prisoners. Danry, Thorin, and Maréchal are quite mad, according to the particulars furnished to me, and the two first gave indubitable marks of madness in my presence."

In consequence, Danry was transferred to Charenton on September 27, 1775, "on account of mental derangement, in virtue of a royal order of the 23rd of the said month, countersigned by Lamoignon. The king will pay for his keep." On entering his new abode, Latude took the precaution to change his name a third time, and signed the register "Danger."

In passing from the fortress of Vincennes to the hospital of Charenton, Danry thought it was as well to rise still higher in dignity. So we see him henceforth styling himself "engineer, geographer, and royal pensioner at Charenton."

His situation was sensibly changed for the better. He speaks of the kindnesses shown him by the Fathers of La Charité.[1] He had companions whose society pleased him. Halls were set apart for billiards, backgammon, and cards. He had company at his meals and in his walks. He met Allègre, his old fellow-prisoner, whom he came upon among the dangerous lunatics in the dungeons; Allègre had been removed in 1763 from the Bastille, where he was shattering and destroying everything. His latest fancy was that he was God. As to Danry, he had taken so kindly to his rôle as nobleman that to see his aristocratic and well-to-do air, to hear his conversation,

[1] Charenton was under the direction of a religious order known as the *Frères de la Charité*, who undertook the care of sick and weak-minded poor.—T.

full of reminiscences of his family and his early life, no one could have doubted that he actually was the brilliant engineer officer he set up for, who had fallen in the prime of life a victim to the intrigues of the favourite. He hobnobbed with the aristocratic section of society at Charenton and struck up an intimacy with one of his associates, the Chevalier de Moyria, son of a lieutenant-colonel, and a knight of Saint-Louis.

Meanwhile the Parlement, which sent a commission every year to inspect the Charenton asylum—a commission before which Danry appeared on two separate occasions—did not decide that he ought to be set at liberty. But one fine day in September, 1776, the prior of the Fathers, who took a quite exceptional interest in the lot of his pensioner, meeting him in the garden, said to him abruptly : " We are expecting a visit from the lieutenant of police ; get ready a short and taking address to say to him." The lieutenant of police, Lenoir, saw Danry, and listened to him attentively, and as the prior's account of him was entirely favourable, the magistrate promised him his liberty. "Then Father Prudentius, my confessor, who was behind me, drew me by the arm to get me away, fearing lest, by some imprudent word, I might undo the good that had been decided on "—a charming incident, much to the honour of Father Prudentius.

But on consideration it appeared dangerous to fling so suddenly upon society a man who would be at a loss how to live, having neither relatives nor fortune, having no longer the means of gaining a livelihood, and a man, moreover, whom there was only too much reason to mistrust. Lenoir asked the prisoner if, once set at liberty, he would find the wherewithal to assure his existence; if he had any property; if he could give the names of any persons willing to go bail for him.

What did this mean—*if* he had any property, *if* he could find sureties? He, Masers de Latude! Why, his whole family, when the Marquise de Pompadour had him put in the Bastille, was occupying a brilliant position! Why, his mother, of whose death he had had the agony to hear, had left a house and considerable estates! Latude took his pen, and without hesitation wrote to M. Caillet, royal notary at Montagnac: " My dear friend, I would bet ten to one you believe me dead; see how mistaken you are! . . . You have but to say the word and before the carnival is over we shall eat a capital leveret together." And he speaks to his friend the notary of the fortune left by his mother, and of his family, who all of them cannot fail to be interested in him. Latude himself was not greatly astonished at receiving no reply to this epistle : but it must have passed under the eyes of the lieutenant of police, and what more did he want?

Latude's new friend, the Chevalier de Moyria, had already been for some time at liberty. The prisoner hastened to send him a copy of his letter to the notary. "The reply is a long time coming, M. Caillet is dead, doubtless." What is to become of him? These twenty-eight years of captivity have endangered his fortune, have made him lose his friends ; how is he to find the remnant of his scattered family? Happily there remains to him a friendship, a friendship still recent, but already strong, in which he places his whole confidence. "Chevalier, it would only need your intervention to deliver me, by inducing your good mother to write to M. Lenoir." The Chevalier de Moyria sent an amiable reply. Danry wrote another and more urgent letter, with such success that not only the Chevalier's mother, but also an old friend of the Moyria family, Mercier de Saint-Vigor, a colonel, and controller-general of the queen's household, intervened, and made applications at Versailles. "On June 5, 1777, King Louis XVI. restored to me my freedom; I have in my pocket the warrant under his own hand!"

On leaving Charenton, Danry signed an undertaking to depart immediately for Languedoc, an undertaking which he did not trouble to fulfil. Paris was the only city in France where a man of his stamp could thrive. He was now fifty-two years old, but was still youthful in appearance, full of go and vigour; his hair, as abundant as it had been in youth, had not become white. He soon found means of borrowing some money, and then we see him opening a campaign, exerting himself to get in touch with the ministers, gaining the protection of the Prince de Beauvau, distributing memorials in which he claimed a reward for great services rendered, and launched out into invectives against his oppressors, Sartine in particular. Minister Amelot sent for him, and in tones of severity notified him that he was to leave the city at once. Latude did not wait for the command to be repeated. He had reached Saint-Bris, about a hundred miles from the capital, when he was suddenly arrested by the police officer Marais. Brought back to Paris, he was locked up in the Châtelet on July 16, 1777, and on August 1 conducted to Bicêtre. The first use he had made of his liberty was to introduce himself to a lady of quality and extort money from her by menaces. The officer found a considerable sum in his possession.

Bicêtre was not a state prison like the Bastille and Vincennes, or an asylum like Charenton; it was the thieves' prison. On entering, Danry took the precaution of changing his name a fourth time, calling himself Jedor. He is, moreover, careful in his *Memoirs* to give us the reason of this fresh metamorphosis: "I would not sully my father's name by inscribing it on the register of this infamous place." From this day there begins for him a truly wretched existence; huddled with criminals, put on bread and water, his lodging is a cell. But his long martyrdom is nearing its end: the hour of his apotheosis is at hand!

Louis XVI. had now been on the throne for several years, and France had become the most impressionable country in the world. Tears flowed at the slightest provocation. Was it the sentimental literature, which Rousseau made fashionable, that produced this moving result, or contrariwise, was the literature successful because it hit the taste of the day? At all events, the time was ripe for Latude. His recent unlucky experience was not to dishearten him. On the contrary, it is with a greater energy, a more poignant emotion, and cries still more heartrending, that he resumes the story of his interminable sufferings. The victim of cruel oppressors, of cowardly foes who have their own reasons for smothering his voice, he will not bend his head under his abominable treatment; he will remain proud, self-assured, erect before those who load him with irons!

On the birth of the Dauphin, Louis XVI. resolved to admit his wretched prisoners to a share of his joy and to pronounce a great number of pardons. A special commission, composed of eight counsellors of the Châtelet and presided over by Cardinal de Rohan, sat at Bicêtre. Danry appeared before it on May 17, 1782. His new judges, as he testifies, heard his story with interest. But the decision of the commission was not favourable to him. He was not so much surprised at this as might be supposed: "The impure breath of vice," he wrote to the Marquis de Conflans, "has never tainted my heart, but there are magistrates who would let off guilty men with free pardons rather than expose themselves to the merited reproach of having committed injustice of the most revolting kind in keeping innocence for thirty-three years in irons."

Giving rein to the marvellous activity of his brain, he composed at Bicêtre new schemes, memorials, and accounts of his misfortunes. To the Marquis de Conflans he sends a scheme for a hydraulic press, "the homage of an unfortunate nobleman who has grown old in irons"; he induces the turnkeys to carry memorials to all who may possibly interest themselves in him. The first to take compassion on him was a priest, the Abbé Legal, of the parish of St. Roch, and curate of Bicêtre. He visited him, consoled him, gave him money, showed him attentions. Cardinal de Rohan also took much interest in him, and sent him some assistance through his secretary. We are coming at last to Madame Legros. This wonderful story is so well known that we shall tell it briefly. A drunken turnkey chanced to lose one of Latude's memorials at a corner of the Rue des Fossés-Saint-Germain-l'Auxerrois: it was picked up and opened by a woman, a haberdasher in a small way. Her heart burned within her as she read of these horrible sufferings, depicted in strokes of fire. She inspired her husband with her own emotion; henceforth it was to be the aim in life of these worthy people to effect the unhappy man's deliverance, and Madame Legros devoted herself to the self-imposed task with indefatigable ardour, courage, and devotion. "A grand sight," cries Michelet, "to see this poor, ill-clad woman going from door to door, paying court to footmen to win entrance into mansions, to plead her cause before the great, to implore their support!" In many houses she was well received. President de Gourgues, President de Lamoignon, Cardinal de Rohan, aided her with their influence. Sartine himself took steps on behalf of the unhappy man. Two advocates of the Parlement of Paris,

Lacroix and Comeyras, devoted themselves to his cause. Copies were made of the prisoner's memorials and distributed in every drawing-room; they penetrated even into the boudoir of the queen. All hearts were stirred by the accents of this harrowing voice.

The Marquis de Villette, who had become celebrated through the hospitality he showed to Voltaire when dying, conceived a passionate enthusiasm for Danry. He sent his steward to Bicêtre to offer him a pension of 600 livres on the sole condition of the prisoner's leaving his case entirely in the Marquis's hands. Latude received this singular proposal with becoming dignity. "For two years a poor woman has been devoting herself to my cause. I should be an ungrateful wretch if I did not leave my fate in her hands." He knew that this pension would not escape him, and it was not for 600 livres that he would have consented to rob his story of the touching and romantic features it was increasingly assuming.

Further, the French Academy actually intervenes! D'Alembert is all fire and flame. From this time a stream of visitors of the highest distinction flows through the squalid prison. At length the king himself is led to look into the affair. He has the documentary evidence brought to him and examines it carefully. With what anxiety everyone awaits his decision! But Louis XVI., now acquainted with the case, replies that Latude will be released—*never!* At this decree, to all appearance irrevocable, all the prisoner's friends lose heart, except Madame Legros. The queen and Madame Necker are on her side. In 1783, Breteuil, the queen's man, comes into power; on March 24, 1784, the release is signed! The Vicomte de Latude receives a pension of 400 livres, but is exiled to his own part of the country. New importunities, new applications; at last they succeed: Latude is free to live in Paris!

This is the grandest period in the life of a great man! Latude is soon in occupation of a modest but decent and well-ordered suite of rooms on the fourth floor. He lives with his two benefactors, M. and Madame Legros, petted, spoilt in a thousand ways. The Duchess of Beauvau has obtained for Madame Legros from Calonne, out of funds intended for the support of distressed gentlefolk, a pension of 600 livres: the Duchess of Kingston[1] grants a pension of the same amount. In addition to the royal pension, Latude receives 500 livres a year from President Dupaty and 300 from the Duke d'Ayen. Moreover, a public subscription is opened, and the list is filled with the greatest names in France. An agreeable competency is assured to the Legros couple and their adopted son. At its sitting on March 24, the French Academy

[1] This was Elizabeth Chudleigh (1720—1788), the notorious beauty who privately married the Hon. Augustus Hervey, afterwards Earl of Bristol, separated from him after three years, and became the mistress of the second Duke of Kingston, whom she bigamously married. After his death she was tried by the House of Lords for bigamy, and fled to France to escape punishment. Her gallantries and eccentricities were the talk of Europe.—T.

solemnly awarded the Montyon prize to the valiant little haberdasher. "The Dame Legros came to receive the medal amid the acclamations of the whole assembly."

The name of Latude is on everyone's lips; he wins admiration and pity on all sides. Ladies of the highest society are not above mounting to the fourth story, accompanied by their daughters, to bring the poor man "aid in money, with their tears." The hero has left a complacent description of the throng: duchesses, marchionesses, grandees of Spain, wearers of the cross of St. Louis, presidents of the Parlement, all these met at his house. Sometimes there were six or eight persons in his room. Everyone listened to his story and lavished on him marks of the most affectionate compassion, and no one failed before going away "to leave a mark of his sensibility." The wives of Marshals de Luxembourg and de Beauvau, the Duchess de la Rochefoucauld, the Countess de Guimont, were among the most zealous. "Indeed," says our hero, " it would be extremely difficult for me to tell which of these countesses, marchionesses, duchesses, and princesses had the most humane, the most compassionate heart."

Thus Latude became one of the lions of Paris: strangers flocked to his lodging, hostesses ran off with him. At table, when he spoke, all voices were hushed with an air of deference and respect; in the drawing-room you would find him seated in a gilt chair near the fireplace where great logs were blazing, and surrounded by a thick cluster of bright, silky, rustling robes. The

Chevalier de Pougens, son of the Prince de Conti, pressed him to come and stay at his house ; Latude graciously consented. The American ambassador, the illustrious Jefferson, invited him to dinner.

Latude has himself described this enchanted life: "Since I left prison, the greatest lords of France have done me the honour of inviting me to eat with them, but I have not found a single house—except that of the Comte d'Angevillier, where you could meet men of wit and learning in scores, and receive all sorts of civilities on the part of the countess ; and that of M. Guillemot, keeper of the royal palaces, one of the most charming families to be found in Paris—where you are more at your ease than with the Marquis de Villette.

"When a man has felt, as I have felt, the rage of hunger, he always begins by speaking of his food. The Marquis de Villette possesses a cook who is a match for the most skilful in his art : in a word, his table is first-rate. At the tables of the dukes and peers and marshals of France there is eternal ceremony, and everyone speaks like a book, whereas at that of the Marquis de Villette, men of wit and learning always form the majority of the company. All the first-class musicians have a cover set at his table, and on at least three days of the week he gives a little concert."

On August 26, 1788, died one of the benefactresses of Latude, the Duchess of Kingston, who did not fail to mention her protégé in her will. We see him dutifully assisting at the sale of the lady's furniture and effects.

He even bought a few things, giving a *louis d' or* in payment. Next day, the sale being continued, the auctioneer handed the coin back to Latude: it was bad. Bad! What! did they take the Vicomte de Latude for a sharper? The coin bad! Who, he would like to know, had the insolence to make "an accusation so derogatory to his honour and his reputation?" Latude raised his voice, and the auctioneer threatened to bundle him out of the room. The insolent dog! "Bundle out rogues, not gentlemen!" But the auctioneer sent for the police, who put "the Sieur de Latude ignominiously outside." He went off calmly, and the same day summoned the auctioneer before the Châtelet tribunal, "in order to get a reparation as authoritative as the defamation had been public."

In the following year (1789) Latude made a journey into England. He had taken steps to sue Sartine, Lenoir, and the heirs of Madame de Pompadour in the courts in order to obtain the damages due to him. In England, he drew up a memorandum for Sartine, in which he informed the late lieutenant of police of the conditions on which he would withdraw his actions. "M. de Sartine, you will give me, as compensation for all the harm and damage you have made me suffer unjustly, the sum of 900,000 livres; M. Lenoir, 600,000 livres; the heirs of the late Marquise de Pompadour and Marquis de Menars, 100,000 crowns; in all, 1,800,000 livres;" that is to say, about £160,000 in English money of to-day.

LATUDE.
From the Painting by Vestier (Hôtel Carnavalet).

The Revolution broke out. If the epoch of Louis XVI., with its mildness and fellow-feeling, had been favourable to our hero, the Revolution seems to have been ordained on purpose for him. The people rose against the tyranny of kings: the towers of the Bastille were overthrown. Latude, the victim of kings, the victim of the Bastille and arbitrary warrants, was about to appear in all his glory.

He hastened to throw into the gutter his powdered peruque and viscount's frock; listen to the revolutionist, fierce, inflexible, indomitable, uncompromising: "Frenchmen, I have won the right to tell you the truth, and if you are free, you cannot but love to hear it.

"For thirty-five years I meditated in dungeons on the audacity and insolence of despots; with loud cries I was calling down vengeance, when France in indignation rose up as one man in one sublime movement and levelled despotism with the dust. The will to be free is what makes a nation free; and you have proved it. But to preserve freedom a nation must make itself worthy of it, and that is what remains for you to do!"

In the Salon of 1789 there were two portraits of Latude with the famous ropeladder. Below one of these portraits, by Vestier, a member of the Royal Academy, these lines were engraved:—

> Instruit par ses malheurs et sa captivité
> A vaincre des tyrans les efforts et la rage,
> Il apprit aux Français comment le vrai courage
> Peut conquérir la liberté.[1]

[1] Instructed by his misfortunes and his captivity how to vanquish the efforts and the rage of tyrants, he taught the French how true courage can win liberty.

In 1787 the Marquis de Beaupoil-Saint-Aulaire had written, inspired by Latude himself, the story of the martyr's captivity. Of this book two editions appeared in the same year. In 1789 Latude published the narrative of his escape from the Bastille, as well as his *Grand Mémoire* to the Marquise de Pompadour; finally, in 1790 appeared *Despotism Unmasked, or the Memoirs of Henri Masers de Latude*, edited by the advocate Thiéry. The book was dedicated to La Fayette. On the first page we see a portrait of the hero, his face proud and energetic, one hand on the ropeladder, the other extended towards the Bastille which workmen are in the act of demolishing. "I swear," says the author at the commencement, "that I will not relate one fact which is not true." The work is a tissue of calumnies and lies; and what makes a most painful impression on the reader is to see this man disowning his mother, forgetting the privations she endured out of love for her son, and ascribing the credit of what little the poor thing could do for her child to a Marquis de la Tude, knight of St. Louis, and lieutenant-colonel of the Orleans Dragoons!

But the book vibrates with an incomparable accent of sincerity and of that profound emotion which Latude knew so well how to infuse into all those with whom he had to do. In 1793, twenty editions had been exhausted, the work had been translated into several languages; the journals had no praise strong enough for the boldness and genius of the author; the *Mercure de France* proclaimed that henceforth it was a parent's duty to teach his children to read in this sublime work ; a copy was sent to all the departments, accompanied by a model of the Bastille by the architect Palloy. With good reason could Latude exclaim in the National Assembly : " I have not a little contributed to the Revolution and to its consolidation."

Latude was not the man to neglect opportunities so favourable. To begin with, he sought to get his pension augmented, and presented to the Constituent Assembly a petition backed by representative Bouche. But Camus, " rugged Camus," president of the committee appointed to investigate the matter, decided on rejection ; and at the sitting of March 13, 1791, deputy Voidel delivered a very spirited speech ; his view was that the nation had unhappy folk to succour more worthy of their concern than a man whose life had begun with roguery and villainy. The Assembly sided with him ; not only was Latude's pension not increased, but on consideration, the pension granted by Louis XVI. was altogether withdrawn.

Horror and infamy ! " What madness has seized on the minds of the representatives of the most generous nation in the world ! . . . To slay a hapless wretch the mere sight of whom awakens pity and warms into life the most sluggish sensibility . . . for death is not so terrible as the loss of honour ! " The valiant Latude will not abide the stroke of such an insult. Ere long he has brought Voidel to retract ; in the heart of the Assembly he gains an influential supporter in the Marshal de Broglie. The Constituent Assembly is replaced by the Legislative, and Latude returns to the charge. He is admitted to the bar of the House on January 26, 1792; the matter is re-committed and gone into a second time on February 25. We should like to be able to quote at length the speech which Latude himself composed for his advocate; here is a portion of the peroration:—

"That a man, without any outside assistance, should have been able to escape three times, once from the Bastille and twice from Vincennes, yes, gentlemen, I venture to say he could not have succeeded except by a miracle, or else that Latude has more than extraordinary genius. Cast your eyes on this ladder of rope and wood, and on all the other instruments which Latude constructed with a mere knife, which you see here in the centre of this chamber. I resolved to bring before your own eyes this interesting object, which will for ever win admiration from men of intelligence. Not a single stranger comes to Paris without going to see this masterpiece of intelligence and genius, as well as his generous deliverer, Madame Legros. We have resolved to give you, gentlemen, the pleasure of seeing this celebrated woman, who unremittingly for forty months set despotism at defiance, and vanquished it by dint of virtue. Behold her there at the bar with M. de Latude, behold that incomparable woman, for ever to be the glory and the ornament of her sex!"

It is not surprising that the Legislative Assembly was

deeply moved by this eloquent harangue and this exhibition of the lady, as touching as unexpected. It unanimously voted Latude a pension of 2000 livres, without prejudice to the pension of 400 livres previously awarded. Henceforth Latude will be able to say : " The whole nation adopted me ! "

However, the little mishap in the Constituent Assembly was to be the only check that Latude suffered in the course of his glorious martyr's career. Presented to the Society of " Friends of the Constitution," he was elected a member by acclamation, and the Society sent a deputation of twelve members to carry the civic crown to Madame Legros. The leader of the deputation said, in a voice broken by emotion, " This day is the grandest day of my life." A deputation from the principal theatres of Paris offered Latude free admission to all performances, " so that he might go often and forget the days of his mourning." He was surrounded by the highest marks of consideration ; pleaders begged him to support their cases before the tribunals with the moral authority bestowed on him by his virtue. He took advantage of this to bring definitively before the courts his claims against the heirs of the Marquise de Pompadour. Citizen Mony argued the case for the first time before the court of the sixth arrondissement on July 16, 1793 ; on September 11 the case came again before the magistrates : Citizens Chaumette, Laurent, and Legrand had been designated by the Commune of Paris as counsel for the defence, and the whole Commune was present at the hearing.

Latude obtained 60,000 livres, 10,000 of which were paid him in cash.

And now his life became more tranquil. Madame Legros continued to lavish her care on him. The 50,000 livres remaining due to him from the heirs of the Marquise were paid in good farm lands situated in La Beauce, the profits of which he regularly drew.

Let us hasten to add that France did not find in Latude an ungrateful child. The critical situation in which the nation was then struggling pained him deeply. He sought the means of providing a remedy, and in 1799 brought out a "Scheme for the valuation of the eighty departments of France to save the Republic in less than three months," and a "Memoir on the means of re-establishing the public credit and order in the finances of France."

When the estates of Madame de Pompadour were sequestrated, the farms Latude had received were taken from him; but he induced the Directory to restore them. He was less fortunate in his requisition for a licence for a theatre and a gaming-house. But he found consolation. The subsidies he went on extorting from right and left, the proceeds of his farms, the sale of his books, and the money brought in by the exhibition of his ropeladder, which was exhibited by a showman in the different towns of France and England, provided him with a very comfortable income.

The Revolution became a thing of the past. Latude hailed the dawning glory of Bonaparte, and when

Bonaparte became Napoleon, Latude made his bow to the emperor. We have a very curious letter in which he marks out for Napoleon I. the line of conduct he should pursue to secure his own welfare and the good of France. It begins as follows :—

"SIRE,—I have been five times buried alive, and am well acquainted with misfortune. To have a heart more sympathetic than the common run of men it is necessary to have suffered great ills. . . . At the time of the Terror I had the delightful satisfaction of saving the lives of twenty-two poor wretches. . . . To petition Fouquet d'Etinville on behalf of the royalists was to persuade him that I was one myself. When I braved death in order to save the lives of twenty-two citizens, judge, great Emperor, if my heart can do ought but take great interest in you, the saviour of my beloved country."

We are given some details of the last years of Latude's life in the *Memoirs* of his friend, the Chevalier de Pougens, and in the *Memoirs* of the Duchess d'Abrantès. The Chevalier tells us that at the age of seventy-five years he still enjoyed good health; he was "active and gay, and appeared to enjoy to the full the delights of existence. Every day he took long walks in Paris without experiencing the least fatigue. People were amazed to find *no trace* of the cruel sufferings he had undergone in the cells during a captivity of thirty-five years." His popularity suffered no diminution under the Empire. Junot awarded him a pension from funds at his disposal.

One day the general presented him to his wife, along with Madame Legros, whose side Latude never left. "When he arrived," says the Duchess d'Abrantès, "I went to greet him with a respect and an emotion that must have been truly edifying. I took him by the hand, conducted him to a chair, and put a cushion under his feet; in fact, he might have been my grandfather, whom I could not have treated better. At table I placed him on my right. But," adds the Duchess, "my enchantment was of short duration. He talked of nothing but his own adventures with appalling loquacity."

At the age of eighty, a few months before his death, Latude wrote in the most familiar terms to his protector, the Chevalier de Pougens, a member of the Institute: "Now I assure you in the clearest possible words, that if within ten days of the present time, the 11th Messidor, you have not turned up in Paris (the Chevalier was staying at his country estate), I shall start the next day and come to you with the hunger of a giant and the thirst of a cabby, and when I have emptied your cellar and eaten you out of house and home you will see me play the second act of the comedy of *Jocrisse*[1]; you will see me run off with your plates, and dishes, and tankards,

---

[1] Jocrisse is the stock French type of the booby, and as such is a character in many comedies. He breaks a plate, for instance; his master asks him how he managed to be so clumsy, and he instantly smashes another, saying, "*Just like that!*" His master asks him to be sure and wake him early in the morning; Jocrisse answers: "Right, sir, depend on me; *but of course you'll ring!*"—T.

and bottles—empty, you may be sure—and fling all your furniture out of the window!"

On July 20, 1804, Latude compiled one more circular, addressed to the sovereigns of Europe: the kings of Prussia, Sweden, and Denmark, the Archduke Charles, brother of the Emperor; and to the President of the United States. To each of them he sent a copy of his *Memoirs*, accompanied by the famous scheme for replacing with muskets the pikes with which the sergeants were armed. He explained to each of the sovereigns that as the country he ruled was profiting by this child of his genius, it was only just that he should reap some benefit.

Jean Henri, surnamed Danry, alias Danger, alias Jedor, alias Masers d'Aubrespy, alias De Masers de Latude, died of pneumonia at Paris, on January 1, 1805, aged eighty years.

CHAPTER VII.

THE FOURTEENTH OF JULY.

IN the remarkable book entitled *Paris during the Revolution*, M. Adolphe Schmidt writes: "All the purely revolutionary events, the events of the Fourteenth of July, of October 5 and 6, 1789, were the work of an obscure minority of reckless and violent revolutionists. If they succeeded, it was only because the great majority of the citizens avoided the scene of operations or were mere passive spectators there, attracted by curiosity, and giving in appearance an enhanced importance to the movement." Further on he says: "After the fall of the Gironde,[1] Dutard expressed himself in these terms: 'If, out of 50,000 Moderates, you succeed in collecting a compact body of no more than 3000, I shall be much astonished; and if out of these 3000 there are to be found only 500 who are agreed, and courageous enough to express their opinion, I shall be still more astonished.

---

[1] The Girondists (so called from Gironde, a district of Bordeaux) were the more sober republican party in the Assembly, who were forced by circumstances to join the Jacobins against Louis XVI. With their fall from power in the early summer of 1792 the last hope of the monarchy disappeared.—T.

And these, in truth, must expect to be Septembrised.'[1] 'Twelve maniacs, with their blood well up, at the head of the Sansculotte section,' writes Dutard in another report, 'would put to flight the other forty-seven sections of Paris.' Mercier, after the fall of the Gironde, thus expresses himself in regard to the reign of Terror: 'Sixty brigands deluged France with blood: 500,000 men within our walls were witnesses of their atrocities, and were not brave enough to oppose them.'"

To enable the reader to understand the extraordinary and improbable event which is the subject of this chapter, it would be necessary to begin by explaining the circumstances and describing the material and moral state of things in which it happened; and that, unhappily, would occupy much space. Let us take the two principal facts, see what they led to, and then come to the events of the Fourteenth of July.

For its task of governing France, the royal power had in its hands no administrative instrument, or, at any rate, administrative instruments of a very rudimentary character. It ruled through tradition and sentiment. The royal power had been created by the affection and devotion of the nation, and in this devotion and affection lay its whole strength.

What, actually and practically, were the means of government in the hands of the king? "Get rid of *lettres de cachet*," observed Malesherbes, "and you

---

[1] Referring to the horrible massacres of September, 1792, when about 1400 victims perished.—T.

deprive the king of all his authority, for the *lettre de cachet* is the only means he possesses of enforcing his will in the kingdom." Now, for several years past, the royal power had practically renounced *lettres de cachet*. On the other hand, during the course of the eighteenth century, the sentiments of affection and devotion of which we have spoken had become enfeebled, or at least had changed their character. So it was that on the eve of the Revolution the royal power, which stood in France for the entire administration, had, if the expression may be allowed, melted into thin air.

Below the royal power, the lords in the country, the upper ten in the towns, constituted the second degree in the government. The same remarks apply here also. And unhappily it is certain that, over the greater part of France, the territorial lords had forgotten the duties which their privileges and their station imposed. The old attachment of the labouring classes to them had almost everywhere disappeared, and in many particulars had given place to feelings of hostility.

Thus on the eve of '89 the whole fabric of the state had no longer any real existence: at the first shock it was bound to crumble into dust. And as, behind the fragile outer wall, there was no solid structure—no administrative machine, with its numerous, diverse, and nicely-balanced parts, like that which in our time acts as a buffer against the shocks of political crises,—the first blow aimed at the royal power was bound to plunge the whole country into a state of disorganization and disorder from which the tyranny of the Terror, brutal, blood-stained, overwhelming as it was, alone could rescue it.

Such is the first of the two facts we desire to make clear. We come now to the second. Ever since the year 1780, France had been almost continually in a state of famine. The rapidity and the abundance of the international exchanges which in our days supply us constantly from the remotest corners of the world with the necessaries of life, prevent our knowing anything of those terrible crises which in former days swept over the nations. "The dearth," writes Taine, "permanent, prolonged, having already lasted ten years, and aggravated by the very outbreaks which it provoked, went on adding fuel to all the passions of men till they reached a blaze of madness." "The nearer we come to the Fourteenth of July," says an eye witness, "the greater the famine becomes." "In consequence of the bad harvest," writes Schmidt, "the price of bread had been steadily rising from the opening of the year 1789. This state of things was utilized by the agitators who aimed at driving the people into excesses: these excesses in turn paralyzed trade. Business ceased, and numbers of workers found themselves without bread."

A few words should properly be said in regard to brigandage under the *ancien régime*. The progress of manners and especially the development of executive government have caused it utterly to disappear. The reader's imagination will supply all we have not space to say. He will recollect the lengths of daring to which a man like Cartouche[1] could go, and recall what the forest of Bondy[2] was at the gates of Paris.

So grew up towards the end of the *ancien régime* what Taine has so happily called a spontaneous anarchy. In the four months preceding the capture of the Bastille, one can count more than three hundred riots in France. At Nantes, on January 9, 1789, the town hall was invaded, and the bakers' shops pillaged. All this took place to the cries of "Vive le roi!" At Bray-sur-Seine, on May 1, peasants armed with knives and clubs forced the farmers to lower the price of corn. At Rouen, on May 28, the corn in the market place was plundered. In Picardy, a discharged carabineer put himself at the head of an armed band which attacked the villages and carried off the corn. On all sides houses were looted from roof to cellar. At Aupt, M. de Montferrat, defending himself, was "cut into little pieces." At La Seyne, the mob brought a coffin in front of the house of one of the principal burgesses; he was told to prepare for death, and they would do him the honour to bury him. He escaped, and his house was sacked. We cull these facts haphazard from among hundreds of others.

The immediate neighbourhood of Paris was plunged

---

[1] The French Dick Turpin. Of good education, he formed when quite a youth a band of robbers, and became the terror of France. Like Turpin, he is the subject of dramas and stories.—T.

[2] A forest near Paris, on the line to Avricourt. It was a famous haunt of brigands. There is a well-known story of a dog which attacked and killed the murderer of its master there.—T.

The Fourteenth of July 243

in terror. The batches of letters, still unpublished, preserved in the National Archives throw the most vivid light on this point. Bands of armed vagabonds scoured the country districts, pillaging the villages and plundering the crops. These were the "Brigands," a term which constantly recurs in the documents, and more and more frequently as we approach the 14th of July. These armed bands numbered three, four, five hundred men. At Cosne, at Orleans, at Rambouillet, it was the same story of raids on the corn. In different localities of the environs of Paris, the people organized themselves on a military basis. Armed burghers patrolled the streets against the "brigands." From all sides the people rained on the king demands for troops to protect them. Towns like Versailles, in dread of an invasion by these ruffians, implored the king for protection: the letters of the municipal council preserved in the National Archives are in the highest degree instructive.

At this moment there had collected in the outskirts of Paris those troops whose presence was in the sequel so skilfully turned to account by the orators of the Palais-Royal. True, the presence of the troops made them uneasy. So far were the soldiers from having designs against the Parisians that in the secret correspondence of Villedeuil we find the court constantly urging that they should be reserved for the safeguarding of the adjoining districts, which were every day exposed to attack, and for the safe conduct of the convoys of corn coming up to Versailles and Paris. Bands mustered around the capital. In the first weeks of May, near Villejuif, a troop of from five to six hundred ruffians met intending to storm Bicêtre and march on Saint-Cloud. They came from distances of thirty, forty, and fifty leagues, and the whole mass surged around Paris and was swallowed up there as into a sewer. During the last days of April the shopmen saw streaming through the barriers "a terrific number of men, ill clad and of sinister aspect." By the first days of May, it was noticed that the appearance of the mob had altogether changed. There was now mingled with it "a number of strangers from all the country parts, most of them in rags, and armed with huge clubs, the mere aspect of them showing what was to be feared." In the words of a contemporary, "one met such physiognomies as one never remembered having seen in the light of day." To provide occupation for a part of these ill-favoured unemployed, whose presence everybody felt to be disquieting, workshops were constructed at Montmartre, where from seventeen to eighteen thousand men were employed on improvised tasks at twenty sous a day.

Meanwhile the electors chosen to nominate deputies to the National Assembly had been collecting. On April 22, 1789, Thiroux de Crosne, the lieutenant of police, speaking of the tranquillity with which the elections were being carried on, added: "But I constantly have my eye on the bakers."

On April 23, de Crosne referred to the irritation which was showing itself among certain groups of workmen in the Suburb Saint-Antoine against two manufacturers, Dominique Henriot, the saltpetre-maker, and Réveillon, the manufacturer of wall-papers. Henriot was known, not only for his intelligence, but for his kindliness; in years of distress he had sacrificed a portion of his fortune for the support of the workmen; as to Réveillon, he was at this date one of the most remarkable representatives of Parisian industry. A simple workman to begin with, he was in 1789 paying 200,000 livres a year in salaries to 300 workers; shortly before, he had carried off the prize founded by Necker for the encouragement of useful arts. Henriot and Réveillon were said to have made offensive remarks against the workmen in the course of the recent electoral assemblies. They both denied, however, having uttered the remarks attributed to them, and there is every reason to believe that their denials were genuine.

During the night of April 27 and the next day, howling mobs attacked the establishments of Henriot and Réveillon, which were thoroughly plundered. Commissary Gueullette, in his report of May 3, notes that a wild and systematic devastation was perpetrated. Only the walls were left standing. What was not stolen was smashed into atoms. The "brigands"—the expression used by the Commissary—threw a part of the plant out of the windows into the street, where the mob made bonfires of it. Part of the crowd were drunk; nevertheless they flung themselves into the cellars, and the casks were stove in. When casks and bottles were empty, the rioters attacked the flasks containing colouring matter; this they absorbed in vast quantities, and reeled about with fearful contortions, poisoned. When these cellars were entered next day, they presented a horrible spectacle, for the wretches had come to quarrelling and cutting each other's throats. "The people got on to the roofs," writes Thiroux de Crosne, "whence they rained down upon the troops a perfect hailstorm of tiles, stones, &c.; they even set rolling down fragments of chimneys and bits of timber; and although they were fired upon several times and some persons were killed, it was quite impossible to master them."

The riot was not quelled by the troops until 10 o'clock that night; more than a hundred persons were left dead in the street. M. Alexandre Tuetey has devoted some remarkable pages to Réveillon's affair; he has carefully studied the interrogatories of rioters who were arrested. The majority, he says, had been drunk all day. Réveillon, as is well known, only found safety by taking refuge in the Bastille. He was the only prisoner whom the Bastille received throughout the year 1789.

In the night following these bacchanalian orgies, the agents of the Marquis du Châtelet, colonel of the Gardes Françaises, having crept along one of the moats, "saw a crowd of brigands" collected on the further side of the Trône gate. Their leader was mounted on a table, haranguing them.

We come upon them again in the report of Commissary Vauglenne, quoted by M. Alexandre Tuetey. "On

April 29, Vauglenne took the depositions of bakers, confectioners, and pork butchers of the Marais, who had been robbed by veritable bands of highwaymen, who proceed by burglary and violence ; they may possibly be starving men, but they look and act uncommonly like gentlemen of the road."

Meanwhile, in the garden of the Palais-Royal, Camille Desmoulins was haranguing groups of the unemployed and ravenous outcasts, who were pressing round him with wide glaring eyes. Desmoulins vociferates : " The beast is in the trap; now to finish him ! . . . Never a richer prey has ever been offered to conquerors ! Forty thousand palaces, mansions, châteaux, two-fifths of the wealth of France will be the prize of valour. Those who have set up as our masters will be mastered in their turn, the nation will be purged ! " It is easy to understand that in Paris the alarm had become as acute as in the country ; everyone was in terror of the " brigands." On June 25 it was decided to form a citizen militia for the protection of property. " The notoriety of these disorders," we read in the minutes of the electors, " and the excesses committed by several mobs have decided the general assembly to re-establish without delay the militia of Paris." But a certain time was necessary for the organization of this civil guard. On June 30, the doors of the Abbaye, where some Gardes Françaises had been locked up, some for desertion, others for theft, were broken in by blows from hatchets and hammers. The prisoners were led in triumph to the

Palais-Royal, where they were fêted in the garden. The extent of the disorders was already so great that the government, powerless to repress them, had perforce to grant a general pardon. From that day there was no longer any need to capture the Bastille, the *ancien régime* was lost.

The disturbances at the Palais-Royal, the rendezvous of idlers, light women, and hot-headed fools, were becoming ever more violent. They began to talk of setting fire to the place. If some honest citizen plucked up courage to protest he was publicly whipped, thrown into the ponds, and rolled in the mud.

On July 11, Necker was dismissed from the ministry and replaced by Breteuil. At this time Necker was very popular; Breteuil was not, though he ought to have been, particularly in the eyes of supporters of a revolutionary movement. Of all the ministers of the *ancien régime*, and of all the men of his time, Breteuil was the one who had done most for the suppression of *lettres de cachet* and of state prisons. It was he who had closed Vincennes and the Châtimoine tower of Caen, who had got the demolition of the Bastille decided on, who had set Latude at liberty, and how many other prisoners! who had drawn up and made respected, even in the remotest parts of the kingdom, those admirable circulars which will immortalize his name, by which he ordered the immediate liberation of all prisoners whose detention was not absolutely justified, and laid down such rigorous formalities for the future, that the arbitrary character of *lettres de cachet* may be said to have been destroyed by them. Nevertheless the orators of the Palais-Royal succeeded in persuading many people that the advent of Breteuil to the ministry presaged a "St. Bartholomew of patriots." The agitation became so vehement, the calumnies against the court and the government were repeated with so much violence, that the court, in order to avoid the slightest risk of the outbreak of a "St. Bartholomew," ordered all the troops to be withdrawn and Paris to be left to itself.

Meanwhile, Camille Desmoulins was continuing to thunder forth : "I have just sounded the people. My rage against the despots was turned to despair. I did not see the crowds, although keenly moved and dismayed, strongly enough disposed to insurrection. . . . I was rather lifted on to the table than mounted there myself. Scarcely was I there than I saw myself surrounded by an immense throng. Here is my short address, which I shall never forget : ' Citizens ! there is not a moment to lose. I come from Versailles ; M. Necker is dismissed ; this dismissal is the alarm bell of a St. Bartholomew of patriots ; this evening all the Swiss and German battalions will march from the Champ de Mars to cut our throats. Only one resource remains to us : we must fly to arms ! ' "

The Parisians were in an abject state of fright, but it was not the Swiss and German battalions which terrified them. The author of the *Memorable Fortnight*, devoted heart and soul as he was to the revolutionary movement, acknowledges that during the days from the 12th to the 14th of July, all respectable people shut themselves up in their houses. And while the troops and decent people were retiring, the dregs were coming to the surface. During the night of July 12, the majority of the toll gates, where the town dues were collected, were broken open, plundered, and set on fire. "Brigands," armed with pikes and clubs, scoured the streets, threatening the houses in which the trembling and agitated citizens had shut themselves. Next day, July 13, the shops of the bakers and wine merchants were rifled. "Girls snatched the earrings from women who went by; if the ring resisted, the ear was torn in two." "The house of the lieutenant of police was ransacked, and Thiroux de Crosne had the utmost difficulty in escaping from the bands armed with clubs and torches. Another troop, with murderous cries, arrived at the Force, where prisoners for debt were confined: the prisoners were set free. The Garde-Meuble was ransacked. One gang broke in with their axes the door of the Lazarists, smashed the library, the cupboards, the pictures, the windows, the physical laboratory, dived into the cellar, stove in the wine-casks and got gloriously drunk. Twenty-four hours afterwards some thirty dead and dying were found there, men and women, one of the latter on the point of childbirth. In front of the house the street was full of débris and of brigands, who held in their hands, some eatables, others a pitcher, forcing wayfarers to drink and filling for all and sundry. Wine flowed in torrents." Some had possessed themselves of ecclesiastical robes, which they put on, and in this attire yelled and gesticulated down the street. In the minute books of the electors we read at this date : "On information given to the committee that the brigands who had been dispersed showed some disposition to reassemble for the purpose of attacking and pillaging the Royal Treasury and the Bank, the committee ordered these two establishments to be guarded." On the same day, they luckily succeeded in disarming more than a hundred and fifty of these roisterers, who, drunk with wine and brandy, had fallen asleep inside the Hôtel de Ville. Meanwhile the outskirts of Paris were no safer than the city itself, and from the top of the towers of the Bastille they could see the conflagrations which were started in various quarters.

The organization of the citizen militia against these disorders was becoming urgent. When evening came, the majority of the districts set actively to work. Twelve hundred good citizens mustered in the Petit Saint-Antoine district. It was a motley crew : tradesmen and artisans, magistrates and doctors, writers and scholars, cheek by jowl with navvies and carpenters. The future minister of Louis XVI., Champion de Villeneuve, filled the post of secretary. The twelve hundred citizens, as we read in the minutes, "compelled to unite by the too well founded alarm inspired in all the citizens by the danger which seems to threaten them each individually, and by the imminent necessity of taking prompt measures to avert its effects, considering that a number of individuals, terrified perhaps by the rumours which doubtless evil-disposed persons have disseminated, are traversing, armed and in disorder, all the streets of the capital, and that the ordinary town guard either mingles with them or remains a passive spectator of the disorder it cannot arrest; considering also that the prison of the Force has been burst into and opened for the prisoners, and that it is threatened to force open in the same way the prisons which confine vagabonds, vagrants, and convicts . . . in consequence, the assembled citizens decide to organize themselves into a citizen militia. Every man will carry while on duty whatever arms he can procure, save and except pistols, which are forbidden as dangerous weapons. . . . There will always be two patrols on duty at a time, and two others will remain at the place fixed for headquarters." Most of the other districts imitated the proceedings of the Petit-Saint-Antoine. They sent delegates to the Hôtel des Invalides to ask for arms. The delegates were received by Besenval, who would have been glad to grant them what they requested ; but he must have proper instructions. He writes in his *Memoirs* that the delegates were in a great state of fright, saying that the "brigands" were threatening to burn and pillage their houses. The author of the *Memorable Fortnight* dwells on the point that the militia of Paris was formed in self-defence against the excesses of the brigands. Speaking of the minute book of the Petit-Saint-Antoine district, an excellent authority, M. Charavay,

The Fourteenth of July

writes: "The burgesses of Paris, less alarmed at the plans of the court than at the men to whom the name of *brigands* had already been given, organized themselves into a militia to resist them: that was their only aim. The movement which on the next day swept away the Bastille might perhaps have been repressed by the National Guard if its organization had had greater stability." The fact could not have been better put.

The Hôtel de Ville was attacked, and one of the electors, Legrand, only cleared it of the hordes who were filling it with their infernal uproar by ordering six barrels of powder to be brought up, and threatening to blow the place up if they did not retire.

During the night of July 13, the shops of the bakers and wine-sellers were pillaged. The excellent Abbé Morellet, one of the Encyclopædists, who, as we have seen, was locked up in the Bastille under Louis XV., writes: "I spent a great part of the night of the 13th at my windows, watching the scum of the population armed with muskets, pikes, and skewers, as they forced open the doors of the houses and got themselves food and drink, money and arms." Mathieu Dumas also describes in his *Souvenirs* these ragged vagabonds, several almost naked, and with horrible faces. During these two days and nights, writes Bailly, Paris ran great risk of pillage, and was only saved by the National Guard.

The proceedings of these bandits and the work of the National Guard are described in a curious letter from an English doctor, named Rigby, to his wife. "It was necessary not only to give arms to those one could rely on, but to disarm those of whom little protection could be expected and who might become a cause of disorder and harm. This required a good deal of skill. Early in the afternoon we began to catch a glimpse here and there among the swarms of people, where we saw signs of an irritation which might soon develop into excesses, of a man of decent appearance, carrying a musket with a soldierly air. These slowly but surely increased in number; their intention was evidently to pacify and at the same time to disarm the irregular bands. They had for the most part accomplished their task before nightfall. Then the citizens who had been officially armed occupied the streets almost exclusively: they were divided into several sections, some mounting guard at certain points, others patrolling the streets, all under the leadership of captains. When night came, only very few of those who had armed themselves the evening before could be seen. Some, however, had refused to give up their arms, and during the night it was seen how well founded had been the fears they had inspired, for they started to pillage. But it was too late to do so with impunity. The looters were discovered and seized, and we learnt next morning that several of these wretches, taken redhanded, had been executed." Indeed, the repressive measures of the citizens were not wanting in energy. Here and there brigands were strung up to the lamp-posts, and then despatched, as they hung there, with musket shots.

The author of the *Authentic History*, who left the best of the contemporary accounts of the taking of the Bastille which we possess, says rightly enough : " The riot began on the evening of July 12." There was thus a combination of disorders and "brigandage" in which the capture of the Bastille, though it stands out more prominently than the other events, was only a part, and cannot be considered by itself.

The morning of the Fourteenth dawned bright and sunny. A great part of the population had remained up all night, and daylight found them still harassed with anxiety and alarm. To have arms was the desire of all ; the citizens and supporters of order, so as to protect themselves ; the brigands, a part of whom had been disarmed, in order to procure or recover the means of assault and pillage. There was a rush to the Invalides, where the magazines of effective arms were. This was the first violent action of the day. The mob carried off 28,000 muskets and twenty-four cannon. And as it was known that other munitions of war were deposited in the Bastille, the cry of " To the Invalides ! " was succeeded by the cry " To the Bastille ! "

We must carefully distinguish between the two elements of which the throng flocking to the Bastille was composed. On the one hand, a horde of nameless vagabonds, those whom the contemporary documents invariably style the "brigands"; and, on the other hand, the respectable citizens—these certainly formed the minority—who desired arms for the equipment of the civil guard. The sole motive impelling this band to the Bastille was the wish to procure arms. On this point all documents of any value and all the historians who have studied the matter closely are in agreement. There was no question of liberty or of tyranny, of setting free the prisoners or of protesting against the royal authority. The capture of the Bastille was effected amid cries of "Vive le roi!" just as, for several months past in the provinces, the granaries had been plundered.

About 8 o'clock in the morning, the electors at the Hôtel de Ville received some inhabitants of the Suburb Saint-Antoine who came to complain that the district was threatened by the cannon trained on it from the towers of the Bastille. These cannon were used for firing salutes on occasions of public rejoicing, and were so placed that they could do no harm whatever to the adjacent districts. But the electors sent some of their number to the Bastille, where the governor, de Launey, received the deputation with the greatest affability, kept them to lunch, and at their request withdrew the cannon from the embrasures. To this deputation there succeeded another, which, however, was quite unofficial, consisting of three persons, with the advocate Thuriot de la Rosière at the head. They were admitted as their predecessors had been. Thuriot was the eloquent spokesman, "in the name of the nation and the fatherland." He delivered an ultimatum to the governor and harangued the garrison, consisting of 95 Invalides and 30 Swiss soldiers. Some

THE CAPTURE OF THE BASTILLE.

From an anonymous contemporary painting now in the Hôtel Carnavalet.

thousand men were thronging round the Bastille, vociferating wildly. The garrison swore not to fire unless they were attacked. De Launey said that without orders he could do no more than withdraw the cannon from the embrasures, but he went so far as to block up these embrasures with planks. Then Thuriot took his leave and returned to the Hôtel de Ville, the crowd meanwhile becoming more and more threatening.

"The entrance to the first courtyard, that of the barracks, was open," says M. Fernand Bournon in his admirable account of the events of this day; "but de Launey had ordered the garrison to retire within the enclosure, and to raise the outer drawbridge by which the court of the governor was reached, and which in the ordinary way used to be lowered during the day. Two daring fellows dashed forward and scaled the roof of the guard-house, one of them a soldier named Louis Tournay: the name of the other is unknown. They shattered the chains of the drawbridge with their axes, and it fell."

It has been said in a recent work, in which defects of judgment and criticism are scarcely masked by a cumbrous parade of erudition, that Tournay and his companion performed their feat under the fire of the garrison. At this moment the garrison did not fire a single shot, contenting themselves with urging the besiegers to retire. "While M. de Launey and his officers contented themselves with threats, these two vigorous champions succeeded in breaking in the doors and in lowering the outer drawbridge; then the horde

s

of brigands advanced in a body and dashed towards the second bridge, which they wished to capture, firing at the troops as they ran. It was then for the first time that M. de Launey, perceiving his error in allowing the operations at the first bridge to be managed so quietly, ordered the soldiers to fire, which caused a disorderly stampede on the part of the rabble, which was more brutal than brave; and it is at this point that the calumnies against the governor begin. Transposing the order of events, it has been asserted that he had sent out a message of peace, that the people had advanced in reliance on his word, and that many citizens were massacred." This alleged treachery of de Launey, immediately hawked about Paris, was one of the events of the day. It is contradicted not only by all the accounts of the besieged, but by the besiegers themselves, and is now rejected by all historians.

A wine-seller named Cholat, aided by one Baron, nicknamed La Giroflée, had brought into position a piece of ordnance in the long walk of the arsenal. They fired, but the gun's recoil somewhat seriously wounded the two artillerymen, and they were its only victims. As these means were insufficient to overturn the Bastille, the besiegers set about devising others. A pretty young girl named Mdlle. de Monsigny, daughter of the captain of the company of Invalides at the Bastille, had been encountered in the barrack yard. Some madmen imagined that she was Mdlle. de Launey. They dragged her to the edge of the moat, and gave the garrison to understand by their gestures that they were going to burn her alive if the place was not surrendered. They had thrown the unhappy child, who had fainted, upon a mattress, to which they had already set light. M. de Monsigny saw the hideous spectacle from a window of the towers, and, desperately rushing down to save his child, he was killed by two shots. These were tricks in the siege of strongholds of which Duguesclin would never have dreamed. A soldier named Aubin Bonnemère courageously interposed and succeeded in saving the girl.

A detachment of Gardes Françaises, coming up with two pieces of artillery which the Hôtel de Ville had allowed to be removed, gave a more serious aspect to the siege. But the name of Gardes Françaises must not give rise to misapprehension : the soldiers of the regular army under the *ancien régime* must not be compared with those of the present day. The regiment of Gardes Françaises in particular had fallen into a profound state of disorganization and degradation. The privates were permitted to follow a trade in the city, by this means augmenting their pay. It is certain that in the majority of cases the trade they followed was that of the bully. "Almost all the soldiers in the Guards belong to this class," we read in the *Encyclopédie méthodique*, " and many men indeed only enlist in the corps in order to live on the earnings of these unfortunates." The numerous documents relating to the Gardes Françaises preserved in the archives of the

Bastille give the most precise confirmation to this statement. We see, for example, that the relatives of the engraver Nicolas de Larmessin requested a *lettre de cachet* ordering their son to be locked up in jail, where they would pay for his keep, " because he had threatened to enlist in the Gardes Françaises."

From the fifteen cannon placed on the towers, not a single shot was fired during the siege. Within the château, three guns loaded with grape defended the inner drawbridge; the governor had only one of them fired, and that only once. Not wishing to massacre the mob, de Launey determined to blow up the Bastille and find his grave among the ruins. The Invalides Ferrand and Béquart flung themselves upon him to prevent him from carrying out his intention. " The Bastille was not captured by main force," says Elie, whose testimony cannot be suspected of partiality in favour of the defenders ; " it surrendered before it was attacked, on my giving my word of honour as a French officer that all should escape unscathed if they submitted."

We know how this promise was kept, in spite of the heroic efforts of Elie and Hulin, to whom posterity owes enthusiastic homage. Is the mob to be reproached for these atrocious crimes ? It was a savage horde, the scum of the population. De Launey, whose confidence and kindness had never faltered, was massacred with every circumstance of horror. " The Abbé Lefèvre," says Dusaulx, " was an involuntary witness of his last moments: ' I saw him fall,' he told me, ' without being able to help him; he defended himself like a lion, and if only ten men had behaved as he did at the Bastille, it would not have been taken.'" His murderers slowly severed his head from his trunk with a penknife. The operation was performed by a cook's apprentice named Desnot, "who knew, as he afterwards proudly said, how to manage a joint." The deposition of this brute should be read. It has been published by M. Guiffrey in the *Revue historique*. To give himself courage, Desnot had gulped down brandy mixed with gunpowder, and he added that what he had done was done in the hope of obtaining a medal.

"We learnt by-and-by," continues Dusaulx, "of the death of M. de Losme-Salbray, which all good men deplored." De Losme had been the good angel of the prisoners during his term of office as major of the Bastille: there are touching details showing to what lengths he carried his kindliness and delicacy of feeling. At the moment when the mob was hacking at him, there happened to pass the Marquis de Pelleport, who had been imprisoned in the Bastille for several years; he sprang forward to save him: "Stop!" he cried, "you are killing the best of men." But he fell badly wounded, as also did the Chevalier de Jean, who had joined him in the attempt to rescue the unfortunate man from the hands of the mob. The adjutant Miray, Person the lieutenant of the Invalides, and Dumont, one of the Invalides, were massacred. Miray was led to the Grève, where the mob had resolved to execute him. Struck with fists and clubs, stabbed with knives, he crawled along in his death agony. He expired, "done to death with pin-pricks," before arriving at the place of execution. The Invalides Asselin and Béquart were hanged. It was Béquart who had prevented de Launey from blowing up the Bastille. "He was gashed with two sword-strokes," we read in the *Moniteur*, "and a sabre cut had lopped off his wrist. They carried the hand in triumph through the streets of the city—the very hand to which so many citizens owed their safety." "After I had passed the arcade of the Hôtel de Ville," says Restif de la Bretonne, who has left so curious a page about the 14th of July, "I came upon some cannibals: one—I saw him with my own eyes—brought home to me the meaning of a horrible word heard so often since: he was carrying at the end of a *taille-cime*[1] the bleeding entrails of a victim of the mob's fury, and this horrible top-knot caused no one to turn a hair. Farther on I met the captured Invalides and Swiss: from young and pretty lips—I shudder at it still—came screams of 'Hang them! hang them!'"

Further, they massacred Flesselles, the provost of the guilds, accused of a treacherous action as imaginary as that of de Launey. They cut the throat of Foulon, an old man of seventy-four years, who, as Taine tells us, had spent during the preceding winter 60,000 francs in order to provide the poor with work. They assassinated Berthier, one of the distinguished men of the time. Foulon's head was cut off; they tore Berthier's heart

[1] Literally "cut-top": we have no equivalent in English.—T.

from his body to carry it in procession through Paris—charming touch!—in a bouquet of white carnations. For the fun was growing fast and furious. De Launey's head was borne on a pike to the Palais Royal, then to the new bridge, where it was made to do obeisance three times to the statue of Henri IV., with the words, "Salute thy master!" At the Palais Royal, two of the conquerors had merrily set themselves down at a dining-table in an entresol. As we garnish our tables with flowers, so these men had placed on the table a trunkless head and gory entrails; but as the crowd below cried out for them, they shot them gaily out of the window.

Those who had remained in front of the Bastille had dashed on in quest of booty. As at the pillage of the warehouses of Réveillon and Henriot, and of the convent of the Lazarists, the first impulse of the conquerors was to bound forward to the cellar. "This rabble," writes the author of the *Authentic History*, "were so blind drunk that they made in one body for the quarters of the staff, breaking the furniture, doors, and windows. All this time their comrades, taking the pillagers for some of the garrison, were firing on them."

No one gave a thought to the prisoners, but the keys were secured and carried in triumph through Paris. The doors of the rooms in which the prisoners were kept had to be broken in. The wretched men, terrified by the uproar, were more dead than alive. These victims of arbitrary power were exactly seven in number. Four were forgers, Béchade, Laroche, La Corrège, and

Pujade ; these individuals had forged bills of exchange, to the loss of two Parisian bankers : while their case was being dealt with in regular course at the Châtelet, they were lodged in the Bastille, where they consulted every day with their counsel. Then there was the young Comte de Solages, who was guilty of monstrous crimes meriting death ; he was kept in the Bastille out of regard for his family, who defrayed his expenses. Finally there were two lunatics, Tavernier and de Whyte. We know what immense progress has been made during the past century in the methods of treating lunatics. In those days they locked them up. Tavernier and de Whyte were before long transferred to Charenton, where assuredly they were not so well treated as they had been at the Bastille.

Such were the seven martyrs who were led in triumphant procession through the streets, amid the shouts of a deeply moved people.

Of the besiegers, ninety-eight dead were counted, some of whom had met their death through the assailants' firing on one another. Several had been killed by falling into the moat. Of this total, only nineteen were married, and only five had children. These are details of some interest.

There was no thought of burying either the conquerors or the conquered. At midnight on Wednesday the 15th, the presence of the corpses of the officers of the Bastille, still lying in the Place de Grève, was notified to the commissaries of the Châtelet. In his admirable work

M. Furnand Bournon has published the ghastly report that was drawn up on that night. It is a fitting crown to the work of the great day: "We, the undersigned commissaries, duly noted down the declaration of the said Sieur Houdan, and having then gone down into the courtyard of the Châtelet (whither the corpses had just been carried), we found there seven corpses of the male sex, the first without a head, clothed in a coat, vest, breeches, and black silk stockings, with a fine shirt, but no shoes; the second also without a head, clothed in a vest of red stuff, breeches of nankeen with regimental buttons, blue silk stockings with a small black pattern worked in; the third also headless, clothed in a shirt, breeches, and white cotton stockings; the fourth also headless, clothed in a blood-stained shirt, breeches, and black stockings; the fifth clad in a shirt, blue breeches, and white gaiters, with brown hair, apparently about forty years old, and having part of his forearm cut off and severe bruises on his throat; the sixth clothed in breeches and white gaiters, with severe bruises on his throat; and the seventh, clothed in a shirt, breeches, and black silk stockings, disfigured beyond recognition."

Meanwhile the majority of the victors, the first moments of intoxication having passed, were hiding themselves like men who had committed a crime. The disorder in the city was extreme. "The commissioners of the districts," writes the Sicilian ambassador, "seeing the peril in which the inhabitants were placed before this enormous number of armed men, including brigands and men let out of prison on the previous days, formed patrols of the National Guard. They proclaimed martial law, or rather, they issued one solitary law declaring that whoever robbed or set fire to a house would be hanged. Indeed, not a day passed without five and even as many as ten persons suffering this penalty. To this salutary expedient we owe our lives and the safety of our houses."

More than one conqueror of the Bastille was hanged in this way, which was a great pity, for two days later his glorious brow might have been crowned with laurels and flowers!

It has been said that the Bastille was captured by the people of Paris. But the number of the besiegers amounted to no more than a thousand, among whom, as Marat has already brought to our notice, there were many provincials and foreigners. As to the Parisians, they had come in great numbers, as they always do, to see what was going on. We have this too on the testimony of Marat. "I was present at the taking of the Bastille," writes the Chancellor de Pasquier also: "what has been called the 'fight' was not serious, and of resistance there was absolutely none. A few musket shots were fired to which there was no reply, and four or five cannon shots. We know the results of this boasted victory, which has brought a shower of compliments upon the heads of the so-called conquerors: the truth is that this great fight did not give a moment's uneasiness to the numerous spectators who had hurried up to see the result. Among them there was many a pretty woman; they had left their carriages at a distance in order to approach more easily. I was leaning on the end of the barrier which closed in the garden skirting Beaumarchais' garden in the direction of the Place de la Bastille. By my side was Mdlle. Contat, of the Comédie Française: we stayed to the end, and I gave her my arm to her carriage. As pretty as any woman could be, Mdlle. Contat added to the graces of her person an intelligence of the most brilliant order."

By next day there was quite another story. The Bastille had been "stormed" in a formidable and heroic assault lasting a quarter of an hour. The guns of the assailants had made a breach in its walls. These, it is true, were still standing intact; but that did not signify, the guns had made a breach, unquestionably! The seven prisoners who had been set free had been a disappointment, for the best will in the world could not make them anything but scoundrels and lunatics; some one invented an eighth, the celebrated Comte de Lorges, the white-headed hero and martyr. This Comte de Lorges had no existence; but that fact also is nothing to the purpose: he makes an admirable and touching story. There was talk of instruments of torture that had been discovered: "an iron corslet, invented to hold a man fast by all his joints, and fix him in eternal immobility:" it was really a piece of knightly armour dating from the middle ages, taken from the magazine of obsolete arms which was kept at the Bastille. Some one discovered also a machine "not less destructive, which was brought to the light of day, but no one could guess its name or its special use"; it was a secret printing-press seized in the house of one François Lenormand in 1786. Finally, while digging in the bastion, some one came upon the bones of Protestants who had once been buried there, the prejudices of the time not allowing their remains to be laid in the consecrated ground of the cemetery: the vision of secret executions in the deepest dungeons of the Bastille was conjured up in the mind of the discoverers, and Mirabeau sent these terrible words echoing through France: "The ministers were lacking in foresight, they forgot to eat the bones!"

The compilation of the roll of the conquerors of the Bastille was a laborious work. A great number of those who had been in the thick of the fray did not care to make themselves known: they did not know but that their laurel-crowned heads might be stuck aloft! It is true that these bashful heroes were speedily replaced by a host of fine fellows who—from the moment when it was admitted that the conquerors were heroes, deserving of honours, pensions, and medals—were fully persuaded that they had sprung to the assault, and in the very first rank. The final list contained 863 names.

Victor Fournel in a charming book has sung the epic, at once ludicrous and lachrymose, of the men of the 14th of July. The book, which ought to be read, gives a host of delightful episodes it is impossible to abridge. In the sequel these founders of liberty did not shine either through the services they rendered to the Republic, or through their fidelity to the immortal principles. The Hulins—Hulin, however, had done nobly in trying to save de Launey—the Palloys, the Fourniers, the Latudes, and how many others ! were the most servile lackeys of the Empire, and those of them who survived were the most assiduous servants of the Restoration. Under the Empire, the conquerors of the Bastille tried to secure the Legion of Honour for the whole crew. They went about soliciting pensions even up to 1830, and at that date, after forty-three years, there were still 401 conquerors living. In 1848 the conquerors made another appearance. There was still mention of pensions for the conquerors of the Bastille in the budget of 1874—let us save the ladder, the ladder of Latude !

This is the amusing side of their story. But there is a painful side too : their rivalries with the Gardes Françaises, who charged them with filching the glory from them, and with the "volunteers of the Bastille." The heroes were acquainted with calumny and opprobrium. There were, too, deadly dissensions among their own body. There were the true conquerors, and others who, while they were true conquerors, were nevertheless not true : there were always "traitors" among the conquerors, as well as "patriots." On July 1, 1790, two of the conquerors were found beaten to death near Beaumarchais' garden, in front of the theatre of their exploits. Next day there was a violent quarrel between four conquerors and some soldiers. In December two others were assassinated near the Champs de Mars. Early in 1791 two were wounded, and a third was discovered with his neck in a noose, in a ditch near the military school. Such were the nocturnal doings on the barriers.

It remains to explain this amazing veering round of opinion, this legend, of all things the least likely, which transformed into great men the "brigands" of April, June, and July, 1789.

The first reason is explained in the following excellent passage from *Rabagas*[1]:—

Carle.—But how then do you distinguish a riot from a revolution?
Boubard.—A riot is when the mob is defeated . . . they are all curs. A revolution is when the mob is the stronger: they are all heroes!

During the night of July 14, the Duke de la Rochefoucauld woke Louis XVI. to announce to him the capture of the Bastille. "It's a revolt then," said the king. "Sire," replied the duke, "it is a revolution."

The day on which the royal power, in its feebleness and irresolution, abandoned Paris to the mob, was the day of its abdication. The Parisians attempted to organize themselves into a citizen militia in order to shoot down the brigands. The movement on the Bastille was a stroke of genius on the part of the latter— instinctive, no doubt, but for all that a stroke of genius. The people now recognized its masters, and with its usual facility it hailed the new régime with adulation. "From that moment," said a deputy, "there was an end

[1] A five-act comedy by Victorien Sardou.

of liberty, even in the Assembly; France was dumb before thirty factionaries."

What rendered the national enthusiasm for the conquerors more easy was precisely all those legends to which credence was given, in all sincerity, by the most intelligent people in France—the legends on the horrors of the Bastille and the cruelties of arbitrary power. For fifty years they had been disseminated throughout the kingdom, and had taken firm root. The pamphlets of Linguet and Mirabeau, the recent stupendous success of the *Memoirs of Latude*, had given these stories renewed strength and vigour. Compelled to bow before the triumphant mob, people preferred to regard themselves —so they silenced their conscience—as hailing a deliverer. There was some sincerity in this movement of opinion, too. The same districts which on July 13 took arms against the brigands could exclaim, after the crisis had passed : " The districts applaud the capture of a fortress which, regarded hitherto as the seat of despotism, dishonoured the French name under a popular king."

In his edition of the *Memoirs of Barras*, M. George Duruy has well explained the transformation of opinion. " In the *Memoirs*, the capture of the Bastille is merely the object of a brief and casual mention. Barras only retained and transmits to us one single detail. He saw leaving the dungeons the 'victims of arbitrary power, saved at last from rack and torture and from living tombs. Such a dearth of information is the more likely to surprise us in that Barras was not only a spectator of the event, but composed, in that same year 1789, an account of it which has now been discovered. Now his narrative of 1789 is as interesting as the passage in the *Memoirs* is insignificant. The impression left by these pages, written while the events were vividly pictured in his mind, is, we are bound to say, that the famous capture of the Bastille was after all only a horrible and sanguinary saturnalia. There is no word of heroism in this first narrative: nothing about 'victims of arbitrary power' snatched from 'torture and living tombs'; but on the other hand, veritable deeds of cannibalism perpetrated by the victors. That is what Barras saw, and what he recorded on those pages where, at that period of his life, he noted down day by day the events of which he was a witness. Thirty years slip by. Barras has sat on the benches of the 'Montagne.'[1] He has remained an inflexible revolutionist. He gathers his notes together in view of *Memoirs* he intends to publish. At this time, the revolutionist version of the capture of the Bastille is officially established. It is henceforth accepted that the Bastille fell before an impulse of heroism on the part of the people of Paris, and that its fall brought to light horrible mysteries of iniquity. This legend, which has so profoundly distorted the event, was contemporary with the event itself, a spontaneous fruit of the popular imagination. And Barras, having to speak of the capture in his

[1] The nickname given to the Jacobins, the extreme revolutionists, who sat on the highest seats on the left in the National Assembly.—T.

Memoirs, discovers his old narrative among his papers, and reads it, I imagine, with a sort of stupefaction. What! the capture of the Bastille was no more than that!—and he resolutely casts it aside."

In the provinces, the outbreak had a violent counterpart. "There instantly arose," writes Victor Fournel, "a strange, extraordinary, grotesque panic, which swept through the greater part of France like a hurricane of madness, and which many of us have heard our grandfathers tell stories about under the name of the 'day of the brigands' or 'the day of the fear.' It broke out everywhere in the second fortnight of July, 1789. Suddenly, one knew not whence, an awful rumour burst upon the town or village: the brigands are here, at our very gates: they are advancing in troops of fifteen or twenty thousand, burning the standing crops, ravaging everything! Dust-stained couriers appear, spreading the terrible news. An unknown horseman goes through at the gallop, with haggard cheeks and dishevelled hair: 'Up, to arms, they are here!' Some natives rush up: it is only too true: they have seen them, the bandits are no more than a league or two away! The alarm bell booms out, the people fly to arms, line up in battle order, start off to reconnoitre. In the end, nothing happens, but their terrors revive. The brigands have only turned aside: every man must remain under arms." In the frontier provinces, there were rumours of foreign enemies. The Bretons and Normans shook in fear of an English descent: in

Champagne and Lorraine a German invasion was feared.

Along with these scenes of panic must be placed the deeds of violence, the assassinations, plunderings, burnings, which suddenly desolated the whole of France. In a book which sheds a flood of light on these facts, Gustave Bord gives a thrilling picture of them. The châteaux were invaded, and the owner, if they could lay hands on him, was roasted on the soles of his feet. At Versailles the mob threw themselves on the hangman as he was about to execute a parricide, and the criminal was set free: the state of terror in which the town was plunged is depicted in the journals of the municipal assembly. On July 23, the governor of Champagne sends word that the rising is general in his district. At Rennes, at Nantes, at Saint-Malo, at Angers, at Caen, at Bordeaux, at Strasburg, at Metz, the mob engaged in miniature captures of the Bastille more or less accompanied with pillage and assassination. Armed bands went about cutting down the woods, breaking down the dikes, fishing in the ponds.[1] The disorganization was complete.

Nothing could more clearly show the character of the government under the *ancien régime:* it was wholly dependent on traditions. Nowhere was there a concrete organization to secure the maintenance of order and the

---

[1] Which were the strict preserves of the aristocrats: to fish in them was as great a crime as to shoot a landlord's rabbit was, a few years ago, in England.—T.

enforcement of the king's decrees. France was a federation of innumerable republics, held together by a single bond, the sentiment of loyalty every citizen felt towards the crown. One puff of wind sent the crown flying, and then disorder and panic bewilderment dominated the whole nation. The door was open to all excesses, and the means of checking them miserably failed. Under the *ancien régime*, devotion to the king was the whole government, the whole administration, the whole life of the state. And thus arose the necessity for the domination of the Terror and the legislative work of Napoleon.

THE END.

INDEX

ALLÈGRE, Latude's fellow prisoner, 154, 185-192, 217.
Ameilhon, city librarian, 55.
Argenson, D', 60, 72, 95, 175, 182.
Arsenal library, 55, 56.
Atrocities of the mob, 258-266.
Avedick, Armenian patriarch, 133.

BARRAS, 272.
Bastille, its situation, 47; appearance, 48; repute, 49, 50; archives, 50-56; origin, 57; site, 58; construction, 59, 60; additions to, 61; appearance in later days, 61, 62; early uses, 63; becomes state prison, 63, 64; prisoners, 65; its administration, 66; gradual transformation, 67; character of prisoners, 68, 69; secretary, 70; office of lieutenant of police, 71; his duties, 71, 72; becomes like modern prisons, 77, 78; abolition of torture, 78; duration of prisoners' detention, 80; expenses, 81; plans for altering, 81-83; a *prison de luxe*, 85; treatment of prisoners, 86; the rooms, 87; manner of prisoners' entrance, 88, 89; cells, 92, 93; tower rooms, 93, 94; furniture, 95, 96; examination of prisoners, 96, 97; indemnified if innocent, 98, 99; allowed companions, 100, 101; prison fare, 102-107; clothes, 107, 108; books, 108, 109; exercise, 109; diversions, 109, 110; funerals, 110, 111; liberation, 111, 112; the Iron Mask, 114-146; men of letters, 147-165; capture, 238-272.
Berryer, 175, 176, 178, 184, 188, 189, 193.
Besmaus, de, 70.
Binguet, 171, 179.
Bread riots, 242, 243.
Breteuil, 78, 248.
Brigands, 241, 245, 250.
Burgaud, 135.

CAMPAN, Madame de, 144, 145.
Carutti's theory of Iron Mask, 134.
Cellamare conspiracy, 72, 73.
Character of French government and society, 239-241.
Chevalier, major, 49, 51, 120, 121, 187, 189, 194.
Citizen militia, 251-253.
Clothes of prisoners, 107, 108.
Crosne, de, lieutenant of police, 244-246.

D'AUBRESPY, Jeanneton, 169, 201.
Dauger suggested as Iron Mask, 135.
Desmoulins, 247, 249.
Diderot, 165.
Diversions of prisoners, 109, 110.
Du Junca's journal, 69, 89, 90, 114-116, 122.
Dusaulx, 51.

INDEX

ENCYCLOPÆDIA, 80.
Estrades, Abbé d', 138-142.

FOOD of prisoners, 102-107.
Funerals, 110.

GAMES of prisoners, 101, 102.
Gleichen, baron, 130.
Griffet, Father, 120.

HEISS, Baron, first to suggest true solution of Iron Mask, 136.
Henriot, 245.
Houdon, sculptor, 82.

JULY 14th, 255-276.
Jung's theory of Iron Mask, 134.

KINGSTON, Duchess of, 225, 227.

LA BEAUMELLE, 152-155.
Lagrange-Chancel, 132.
La Reynie, 71.
Latude, 168-237.
Launay, Mdlle. de, see Staal, Madame de.
Launey, de, governor, 256, 258, 260.
Lauzun, 91.
Legros, Madame de, 223-226, 232, 233.
Lenoir, lieutenant of police, 186.
Lettres de cachet, 240.
Lieutenancy of police created, 97.
Linguet, 163-165.
Loiseleur's theory of Iron Mask, 134.
Loquin's theory of Iron Mask, 133.
Losme, de, 261.
Louis XIV. and Iron Mask, 137-140.
Louis XV. and Iron Mask, 144.
Louis XVI. and Iron Mask, 144.
Louvois, 70, 141.

MAISONROUGE, king's lieutenant, 73-76.
Malesherbes, 78, 156, 216.
Man in the Iron Mask, documents, 114-125; legends, 125-136; true solution, 136-146.
Marmontel, 158-163.
Mattioli, the Iron Mask, 136-146.
Maurepas, 144, 173-175.
Mirabeau, 166, 167.
Morellet, 155-158, 253.
Moyria, de, 218-220.

NECKER, 248.

PALATINE, Madame, 125.
Palteau, M. de, 118, 119.
Papon's theory of Iron Mask, 127.
Parlement, 76, 77.
Pensions to prisoners, 98, 99.
Pompadour, Madame de, 173, 206.
Pontchartrain, 69.
Puget, king's lieutenant, 83.

QUESNAY, Dr., 175, 177, 178.

RAVAISSON, librarian, 54, 55, 134.
Register of St. Paul's church, 117, 142, 143.
Regnier's lines, 59.
Renneville's meals, 103, 104.
Réveillon, 245, 246.
Ricarville, companion of the Iron Mask, 123, 124.
Richelieu, Cardinal, 63-66.
Richelieu, Duke de, 76, 129, 130.
Rigby, Dr., 253, 254.
Risings in the provinces, 273.
Rochebrune, commissary, 195.
Rohan, Cardinal de, 222.

SADE, Marquis de, 95.
Saint-Mars, governor, 87, 115-119, 127, 142.
Saint-Marc, detective, 169, 176, 180, 183, 192.
Sartine, de, 49, 202, 203, 207, 210, 215.
Sauvé, Madame de, her dress, 108.
Solages, de, 84.
Staal, Madame de, 73-76, 94, 95, 102.

INDEX

TAULÈS, de, 132.
Tavernier, 106.
Theories on Iron Mask, 125-136.
Thuriot de la Rosière, 256.
Tirmont, companion of Iron Mask, 123, 124.

VIEUX-MAISONS, Madame de, 128.
Villette, Marquis de, 224.
Vinache's library, 109.
Vincennes, 165-167, 180.
Voltaire, 99, 126, 128, 129, 148-152.

www.ingramcontent.com/pod-product-compliance
Lightning Source LLC
Chambersburg PA
CBHW010044090426
42735CB00018B/3381